GUIDE TO BASIC GARMENT ASSEMBLY FOR THE FASHION INDUSTRY

GUIDE TO BASIC GARMENT ASSEMBLY FOR THE FASHION INDUSTRY

JAYNE SMITH

WILEY-BLACKWELL

A John Wiley & Sons, Ltd, Publication

Library of Congress Cataloging-in-Publication Data is available

A catalogue record for this book is available from the British Library.

ISBN 978-1-405-19888-2 (pbk) ISBN 978-1-118-55578-1 (ebk)
ISBN 978-1-118-55577-4 (ebk) ISBN 978-1-118-55579-8 (ebk)

Set in 9.5/13.5 Myriad Pro Light by MPS Limited, Chennai, India
Printed by Markono Print Media, Singapore

CONTENTS

PREFACE

A general understanding of garment assembly techniques is essential knowledge that will allow all fashion and clothing design students to translate design ideas into reality.

Mastery of the skills and intricacies of this subject area can be difficult to acquire by reading alone, therefore videos have been recorded to visually demonstrate essential assembly techniques, such as dart constructions, zip insertions, attaching waistbands, assembling and attaching collars and cuffs. Chapter 6 onwards also cover step by step assembly instructions for each process.

The other chapters cover an understanding of stitches and seams, details of attachments that can be added to the sewing machine which improve the sewing process, an understanding of which needle and thread type to select for a particular application and how to overcome problems when sewing.

The fundamental requirements of fashion design are a sound knowledge of the basics of garment assembly together with an understanding of the garment assembly terms used in the fashion industry. Armed with this basic information and understanding you will be able to create your own garment designs.

ACKNOWLEDGEMENTS

I am grateful to my colleagues at the School of Textiles & Design, Heriot-Watt University – Sandra Darling, Yvonne Caldwell, Theresa Wilkinson and Eleanor Drummond – who assisted with filming, preparing some of the visuals and proofing the contents illustrated in this book and DVD.

CHAPTER 1
INTRODUCTION

A confident understanding of stitch and seam types, together with a sound knowledge of the basics of assembly, is fundamental to the creation of garments. Armed with this information and understanding you will be able to translate your design ideas into reality, your own three-dimensional design creations.

This book and the illustrative videos cover the essential technology required to get you started in garment assembly by developing your understanding of which stitch and seam type to select for a particular fabric and garment type, as well as the knowledge to construct a range of basic techniques to assemble entire garments using the correct components.

Every stage of constructing garment parts, such as inserting a zip, sewing a dart, assembling and attaching a shirt collar, etc., is covered in the subsequent chapters.

Joining fabric by means of sewing dates back to 28,000 BC, with the earliest known sewing tool: a hand crafted needle made from bone with a split head instead of an eye. The sewing machine was not developed until the 1700s but it did not go into mass production until the 1800s. This machine could produce 250 stitches per minute, which equated to the sewing capacity of five people sewing by hand. Today, modern industrial sewing machines are automated and can exceed speeds of 5000 stitches per minute.

This book covers the techniques and tools used to construct garments for today's fashion industry using modern industrial equipment as well as an understanding of how to resolve sewing problems, such as seam pucker, etc., should they arise during the sewing process.

GETTING STARTED

Working with the correct tools is essential: below are some of the key pieces of equipment required:

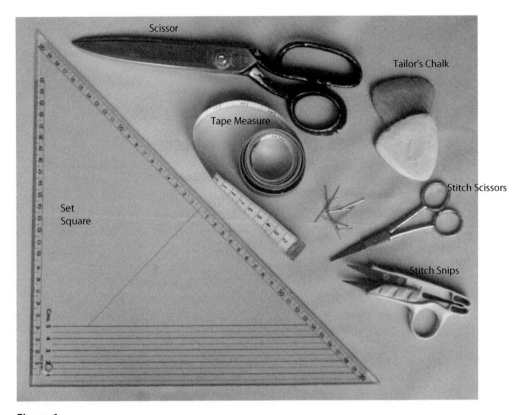

Figure 1

Fabric scissors/shears for cutting fabrics and trimming such as interlining, elastics, etc.

Quality fabric scissors/shears have tempered steel or stainless steel blades that will create an even cut along the entire length of the blade. The blades are joined by a screw, not a rivet, which means that the scissors can be adjusted or repaired if they are damaged.

Fabric shears generally have blades which are more than 6 inches or 15.24cms in length.

Stitch scissors or snips for cutting threads and trimming surplus fabrics during the sewing process.

The tips of both blades should be pointed to enable you to unpick unwanted stitches. The scissors should be easy to handle but large enough to cut through layers of fabric.

Stitch snips are used for unpicking stitching, trimming threads and trimming surplus fabrics.

Tape measure used to accurately measure seam allowances, body and garment dimensions.

The tape should be non-stretchable but flexible with centimetre markings.

Tailor's chalk for marking the garment pieces on the fabric and marking locations which are key to the sewing process.

This chalk will not leave a permanent mark on the fabric; it is used to mark the garment pieces or locations such as dart ends, hem lines, etc. on the fabric. When the marks are no longer required, the chalk marks will brush off, leaving no residue behind.

The most common form of tailor's chalk is a thin triangular shape which can be sharpened and the thin edge is used to mark the fabric. It is also available in the form of a powder with an applicator and in pencil form.

Pins used for temporarily attaching fabric pieces together.

Set square for marking straight lines and cutting strips of fabric for binding.

GETTING TO KNOW THE PARTS OF THE SEWING MACHINE

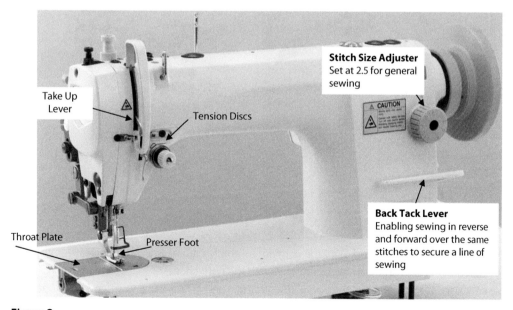

Figure 2

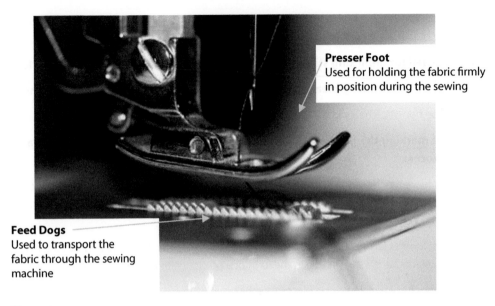

Presser Foot
Used for holding the fabric firmly in position during the sewing

Feed Dogs
Used to transport the fabric through the sewing machine

Figure 3

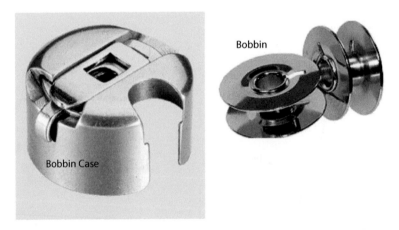

Bobbin

Bobbin Case

Figure 4

The Fashion Designer's understanding of the garment assembly process is key to the creative process. The correct selection of stitch and seam types together with the right choice of thread and interlining to stabilise garment parts are fundamental to good garment design and instrumental to success in the creation of garments.

CHAPTER 2
STITCH & SEAM TYPES

J oining fabric pieces together by sewing produces both strength and flexibility in a seam. Many attempts have been made to develop other processes for joining fabric pieces together, but achieving manufacturing speed and flexibility as well as good seam appearance and performance has proved difficult for many fabric types.

Seams can be joined by a process called welding, as an alternative to sewing. This type of seam joining technology bonds or sticks together fabrics which have a predominant composition of synthetic fibres. The child in the picture is wearing a coat that has been made from lightweight PVC. Welding seams together has limited applications; seams tend to be noticeably stiffer than those that have been joined using traditional stitching methods and seams cannot be welded when the fabric is predominantly made from natural fibres. Generally, welded seams are stronger than conventionally sewn seams because the welding process does not use a needle to create holes in the fabric and weaken the fabric structure. Each section of the welded seam is bonded independently. In conventional seams, if one stitch is broken, the whole seam is compromised, since all the stitches are connected. Many performance waterproof outdoor garments are constructed using a combination of traditional sewing and welding. The seam is sewn with a 5mm seam width, and then has a waterproof tape welded on top, to prevent water from seeping through the holes that have been made in the

Figure 1   The child in the picture is wearing a coat that has been made from lightweight PVC. The seams in this coat have been joined by welding.

fabric by the needle. Welding technology is also used for securing decorative motifs onto garments and neatening the ends of straps made from ribbon.

Seam and stitch types used in garment assembly must perform appropriately with the fabric types used and last throughout the lifetime of the garment. For example, it would be inappropriate to sew a swimsuit made from a knitted stretch Lycra fabric with a stitch type that had limited stretch characteristics, as this would cause the threads in the stitch to snap when the seams in the swimsuit were extended when the garment was worn.

The key characteristics of a seam are as follows.

Appearance

Good appearance in a seam normally means smooth fabric joins with no missing or uneven stitches and no evidence of damage to the material being sewn. Gathers may occur, but this should be a style feature, therefore the amount of gathering and ease should be controlled.

Figure 2 A seam with poor appearance; it has ripples known as seam pucker along the seam length.

Figure 3 A seam which is pucker-free and has a good appearance.

A good seam appearance must be maintained throughout the lifetime of the garment despite damage caused by wear, washing or dry cleaning.

Performance

The seam must achieve the required standards of strength, elasticity, durability, security and comfort. The seam should be as strong as the fabric in both directions. Also, it should stretch and recover with the fabric.

With the increasing use of stretch fabrics in clothing today, the seam must be durable, must not irritate the skin in wear and must not fray or unravel.

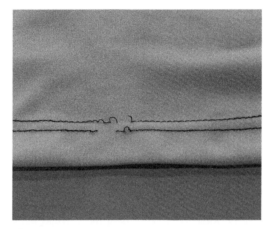

Figure 4

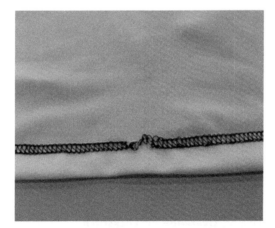

Figure 5

Figures 4 and 5 illustrate a seam where the threads have broken on the hem of a t-shirt that is made from knitted cotton. In this example, the stitch did not perform. The stitch did not stretch as much as the fabric and, as a result, the seam failed.

The fabric and the end use of the garment determine the seam and stitch type that should be used. The needle which is used to pass the thread through the fabric also has to be considered. Needles come in a range of sizes with different points which are only suitable to use when sewing particular fabrics. For example, a needle with a smooth curved point, known as a ball point, should be used when sewing knitted fabrics.

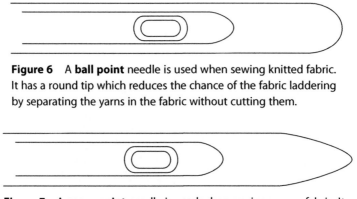

Figure 6 A **ball point** needle is used when sewing knitted fabric. It has a round tip which reduces the chance of the fabric laddering by separating the yarns in the fabric without cutting them.

Figure 7 A **spear point** needle is used when sewing woven fabric. It has a sharp tip which penetrates the fabric.

In the fashion industry, it is the responsibility of the Garment Technologist to evaluate the materials used in the garment and specify the most appropriate and economical assembly process to use.

STITCH TYPES

The British Standards Institution divides stitch types into six classifications, as listed below, and within each classification there are a number of variations known by a specific number.

⇒ Class 100 Single Thread Chainstitches
⇒ Class 200 All Hand stitches
⇒ Class 300 Lockstitches
⇒ Class 400 Multi-thread Chainstitches
⇒ Class 500 Overedge Chainstitches
⇒ Class 600 Covering Chainstitches

The most commonly used stitches are **Overedge** and **Lockstitch**.

Overedge

There are three types of stitch within the Overedge classification. The **Three Thread Overedge** stitch (504), as shown in Figure 8, is used for neatening the edges of woven fabrics and joining seams on garments made from knitted fabrics. The stitch is formed from three threads, one needle thread and two looper threads which lash the edge of the fabric and prevent the fabric edge from fraying.

The Three Thread Overedge stitch (504) is an extensible stitch with excellent recovery properties and is used for neatening and joining seams in garments made from knitted fabrics.

The width of an Overedge stitch is known as the stitch **bight**.

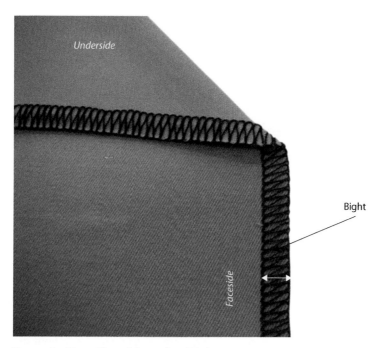

Figure 8   Three Thread Overedge (504).

Owing to the narrow bight, which can vary from 4mm to 6mm, it cannot be used for joining seams on garments made from woven fabrics. This stitch is used for neatening woven fabric edges only.

The **Four Thread Overedge** stitch (514) is formed from four threads, two needle threads and two looper threads which lash the edge of the fabric.

The wider bight, from 6mm to 8mm, enables the stitch to be used for neatening fabric edges and joining seams in garments such as shirts made from lightweight woven fabrics as well as garments made from knitted fabrics, where good seam security is a vital characteristic of the seam.

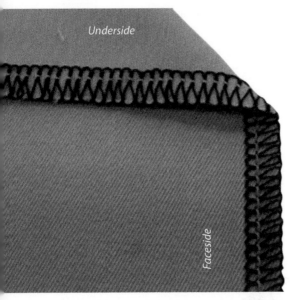

Figure 9   Four Thread Overedge (514).

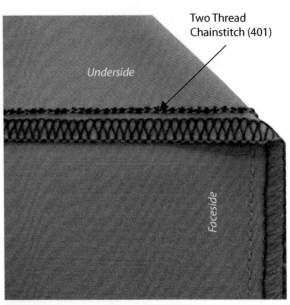

Figure 10   Five Thread Overedge (516).

The **Five Thread Overedge** stitch, frequently known as the Five Thread Safety stitch (516), shown in Figure 10, is used for general seam joining in garments made from **woven fabrics only**.

This stitch is a combination of the Two Thread Chainstitch (401) and Three Thread Overedge (504) and is formed simultaneously on one sewing machine. It both neatens the edge of the fabric and joins the fabric edges together. The stitch cannot be used for joining seams in garments made from stretch fabric as the threads used in the Two Thread Chainstitch (401) will break once the seam is extended.

Lockstitch

Within the Lockstitch classification there are two main stitch types, the Lockstitch (301) and Zig Zag. The **Lockstitch (301)** is used for general joining of seams and topstitching on garments made from woven fabrics. When sewing woven fabrics, it is used for seam joining and attaching components such as a zip, as well as applications such as topstitching, sewing pin tucks and attaching binding to neaten a raw edge on a garment.

The seam is formed from two threads; one needle thread and a bobbin thread which interlace in the middle of the fabric plies being sewn. The stitch appearance is reversible; it is the same on both sides but it has insufficient stretch characteristics for seaming stretch knitted fabrics.

Figure 11 Lockstitch (301).

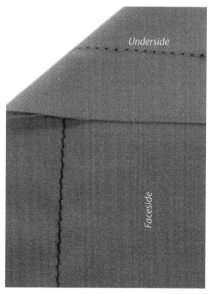

Underside

Faceside

Figure 12

Figure 13

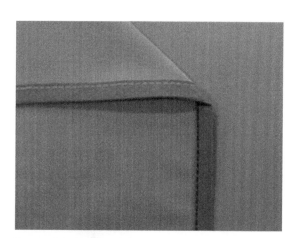

Figure 14 Lockstitch (301).

Figures 13 and 14 show a strip of **woven** fabric, cut on the bias (cross) grain, being applied to the fabric edge using a 301 Lockstitch machine equipped with a folder which folds both raw edges of the binding into the bound edge construction.

Seam Cross-section Diagrams

Seam diagrams which illustrate the fabric configuration in a seam can take quite some time to draw accurately; therefore a simplified version has been established. The simplified diagram shows the cross-section through the fabric which is represented using horizontal lines, and a short vertical line/s represents the point of the needle penetrating the fabric.

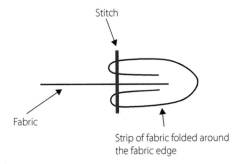

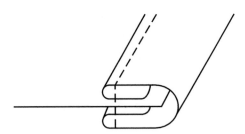

Figure 15   Simplified seam diagram for attaching binding to the fabric edge.

Figure 16

The Zig Zag Lockstitch (304) formation is similar to the 301 Lockstitch, but the Zig Zag formation makes this stitch more extensible and it can be used to sew stretch fabrics with low stretch characteristics. It is used for attaching elastic onto garments such as bras, pants and swimwear.

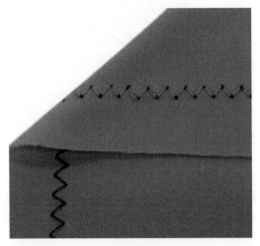

Figure 17   Topstitching using Lockstitch (301).

Figure 18   Zig Zag Lockstitch (304).

Figure 19 A condensed Zig Zag stitch called a **Bar Tack** is used to reinforce weak points on garments, such as the corners of a pocket mouth, and to attach belt loops.

Single Thread Chainstitch

There are two stitches within the Single Thread Chainstitch classification. The **Single Thread Chainstitch (101)** is used for temporary stitching, which is frequently referred to as Basting or Tacking. The Single Thread Chainstitch (101) is used to temporarily sew garments together for fitting purposes before permanent stitching, particularly in tailoring. This stitch is also frequently used to sew decorative effects such as pin tucks.

This stitch is formed from one single thread which is looped around the succeeding loop on the underside of the fabric. The stitch will easily unravel if the end of the row of stitching is not secured.

As shown in Figure 20, the face side of the stitch is different in appearance to the underside.

The **Single Thread Blind stitch (103)** is formed from one single thread and the sewing machine that performs this stitch has a curved needle which partially penetrates the outer fabric and then the hem edge. This secures the hem in position with no visible stitching to the face side of the garment. It is used for securing hems on garments such as trousers, skirts, dresses, unlined jackets and coats.

Figure 20 Single Thread Chainstitch (101).

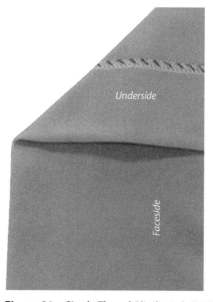

Figure 21 Single Thread Blind stitch (103).

Multi-thread Chainstitch

The **Two Thread Chainstitch (401)** shown in Figure 22 has the appearance of a Lockstitch on the face side but a looped effect on the underside. The threads link on the underside of the fabric therefore reducing the build up of threads in the middle of the fabric, which can alleviate seam pucker in densely woven fabrics. Although the stitch is slightly extensible, it can only be used to join seams made from woven fabrics and the stitch will unravel if the threads are broken.

It is used for joining long seams in garments, such as leg seams on trousers, and sewing lapped seams in garments where good seam strength and durability is critical, therefore it is frequently used in the construction of jeans and work wear garments. A lapped seam is also a decorative seam which is used to join side seams on 'quality' shirts. It is frequently known as a **lapped felled seam,** as shown in Figure 24.

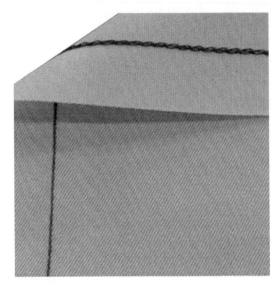

Figure 22

This seam is generally sewn using a twin-needle 401, Two Thread Chainstitch machine equipped with a folder which accurately laps the fabric edges over each other, enclosing them within the seam structure.

Figure 23

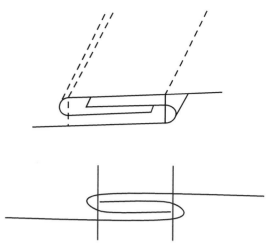

Figure 25 Simplified seam diagram.

Figure 24 Twin-needle Two Thread Chainstitch (401) used to sew a lapped seam.

The **Two Needle Chainstitch Bottom Cover (406)** is used for attaching elastic on briefs, hemming and attaching binding onto garments made from knitted fabrics such as t-shirts.

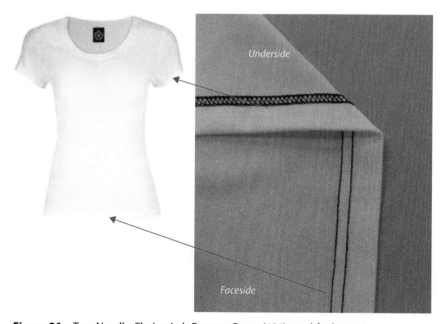

Figure 26 Two Needle Chainstitch Bottom Cover (406) used for hemming.

The stitch is formed from two needle threads passing through the fabric and interlacing with a looper thread on the underside of the fabric.

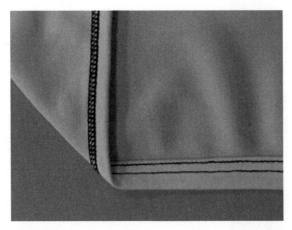

Figure 27   Two Needle Chainstitch Bottom Cover (406) used for attaching binding.

Covering Chainstitches

Stitch types within this classification frequently are called Flatlock stitches. Figure 28 shows the **Two Needle Cover Chainstitch (602),** which is a highly extensible stitch used for attaching elastic or securing hems on

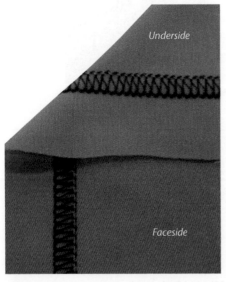

Figure 28   Two Needle Cover Chainstitch (602).

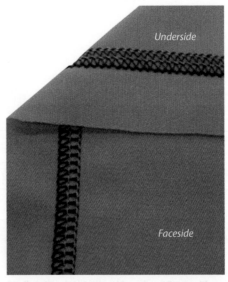

Figure 29   Three Needle Cover Chainstitch (605).

garments made from high stretch fabrics, such as underwear. There are 20cm of thread used in sewing 1cm of seam using this stitch. The stitch is formed from four threads, two needle threads and two looper threads.

The **Three Needle Cover Chainstitch (605)** is a more extensible stitch which is used for joining seams where the fabric edges are butted together or overlapped, and is extensively used in the construction of garments made from stretchy fabrics, such as swimwear, underwear and leisurewear. The stitch is formed from five threads: three needle threads and two looper threads with 27cm of thread used to sew 1cm of the **Three Needle Cover Chainstitch (605)**.

SEAM TYPES

When selecting the appropriate seam type, the following aspects are considered:

Figure 30 Lapped seam.

⇒ The appearance of the seam in the finished garment.
⇒ Strength and durability of the seam. For example, lapped seams are used to sew work wear garments where areas of the garment are subjected to strain when the garment is worn, such as the back seat seam on a pair of jeans.
⇒ The seam should feel comfortable when the garment is worn. For example, smooth, flat seam constructions which do not irritate the skin should be selected when constructing underwear garments.
⇒ Finally, the fabric characteristics will influence the seam selection. For example, French seams are used to sew lightweight fabrics only. The finished seam is pressed flat to one side; to this end, five plies of fabric are superimposed on top of each other; this would give a bulky seam if thick fabrics were used. This is illustrated below in Figures 31 and 32.

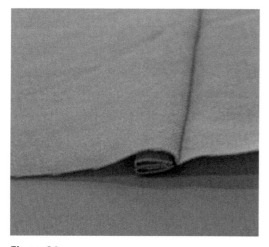

Figure 31

Figure 32

Generally, seams are used for:

⇒ Joining fabric pieces together.

⇒ Neatening raw fabric edges by

   1) hemming
   2) attaching additional trimming or strips of fabric.

Joining Seams

Open Lockstitch seams are used only when a component such as a zip is inserted on garments made from a woven fabric.

Both fabric edges are separately neatened using the Three Thread Overedge stitch, the right sides of the fabric pieces are placed together and joined using the 301 Lockstitch. The seam allowance is then pressed apart using an iron.

Figure 33 Open seam.

Figure 34 Simplified seam diagram.

The French seam can only be used for joining lightweight fabrics for garments such as lingerie, evening wear, dresses, blouses, and skirts. A French seam is a complex seam and is therefore costly to produce and should not be used for joining seams on garments where garment cost is a critical factor. The seam is sewn using the 301 Lockstitch. The plies of fabric are first sewn with the wrong sides of the fabric placed together, and then a second seam is sewn with face sides together, enclosing the raw edges of the fabric within the seam structure.

Figure 36   Simplified seam diagram.

Figure 35   French seam.

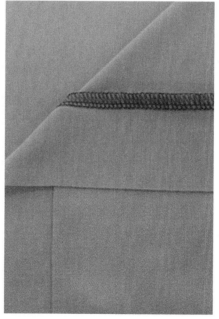

Figure 37   504 Three Thread Overedge.

Figure 38   514 Four Thread Overedge.

Figure 39   516 Five Thread Overedge.

A **closed seam** is an economically constructed seam type used for joining garment pieces together. The face sides of the fabric are placed together and the two plies are stitched together using one of the Overedge stitches.

The Three Thread Overedge (504) is used to create closed seams in garments such as t-shirts, underwear and sportswear made from knitted fabrics.

The Four Thread Overedge (514) closed seam is used for joining seams together when using knitted fabrics where good seam security is a vital characteristic. It can also be used for seaming garments made from lightweight woven fabrics when the seam is not subjected to any strain, such as the side seams on shirts or blouses.

The Five Thread Overedge (516) closed seam is used for seaming garments made from woven fabrics only, such as joining the side seams on skirts, trousers and dresses.

A **lapped seam** as aforementioned is classified as a joining seam. This seam is generally sewn using a twin-needle (401), Two Thread Chainstitch machine equipped with a folder which accurately laps the fabric edges over each other, enclosing them within the seam structure.

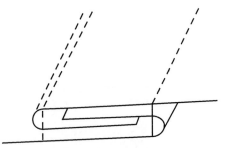

Figure 40   Simplified seam diagram.

Figure 41   Lapped seam.

Figure 42   Simplified seam diagram.

A lapped seam is frequently known as a lapped felled seam. It is used in garments where good seam strength and durability are critical, and is frequently used in the construction of jeans and work wear garments. This seam type is also a decorative seam which is frequently used to join side seams on 'quality' shirts.

Neatening Raw Fabric Edges

There are a variety of different methods that may be used to neaten the lower edge of a garment. The depth of the hem is determined by the garment style, fabric, cost and whether the hem is straight or curved.

A **single turn hem,** as shown in Figure 43, is used for hemming garments made from woven fabrics only. The fabric edge is neatened using the Three Thread Overedge stitch and then the hem is turned over by the desired amount and the hem is secured in position with the Lockstitch (301).

The width of the hem turning is determined by the shape of the fabric edge being hemmed; for example, if the edge of the fabric is curved, the hem allowance turning should be 1cm or less, whereas if the fabric edge is straight, the hem allowance turning can be more substantial.

Figure 43   Single turn hem.

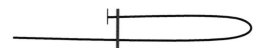

Figure 44   Simplified seam diagram.

In a **double turn hem** the fabric edge is turned over and turned over again then secured in position with the 301 Lockstitch machine which is equipped with a folder to double turn the fabric edge. As described above, the hem turning width is determined by the shape of the fabric edge being hemmed.

Figure 46 Simplified seam diagram.

Figure 45   Double turn hem.

Hems on garments such as trousers, skirts, dresses, unlined jackets and coats can also be neatened using the Single Thread Blind stitch (103), as described on page 13 (Figure 21).

Binding is a decorative method used to finish off a neckline or armholes on garments. Refer to Figure 47.

The hem of a garment made from lightweight flimsy fabric can be difficult to neaten using the methods described previously. With a rolled edge hem, the hem is neatened using the Three Thread Overedge (504). The stitch density is increased and the stitch bight is reduced to approximately 3mm, providing a decorative finished edge.

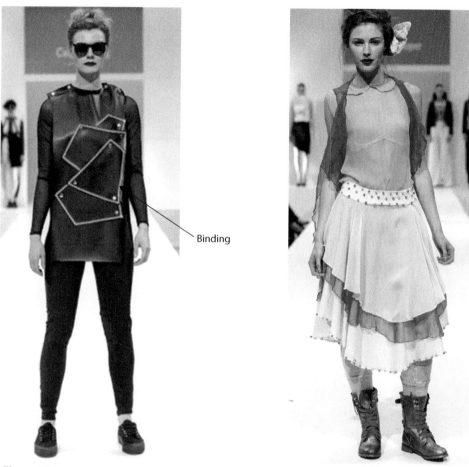

Binding

Figure 47

Figure 49

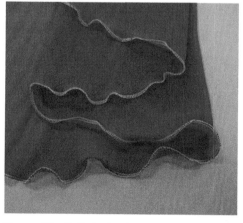

Figure 48 Rolled edge hem using 504 Three Thread Overedge.

CHAPTER 3

ATTACHMENTS FOR THE SEWING MACHINE

A variety of simple attachments can be added to the basic sewing machine, which will assist the machinist to perform sewing tasks faster and more accurately. These attachments are generally referred to as **work aids**; they enable complex sewing tasks to be performed in a less complicated manner, resulting in reduced fatigue.

EDGE GUIDE

When stitching has to be located in a certain position or a particular distance from the edge of the fabric, guides can be added to the bed or presser foot of the sewing machine.

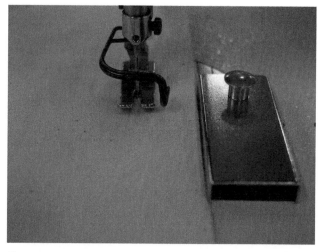

Figure 1

This magnetic **edge guide** forms a physical barrier whereby the edge of the fabric is guided along the barrier, giving accuracy in seam widths.

A '**T**' **guide** can be attached to the sewing machine bed with a screw.

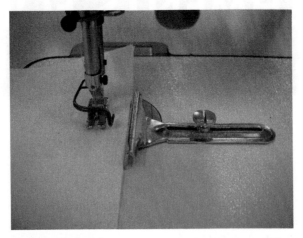

Figure 2   T Guide.

The distance from the edge of the 'T' guide to the presser foot can be adjusted to provide the desired seam width.

The guide below, known as a **swing guide**, can be moved into position when a guide is required for straight stitching along the edge of the fabric, and simply moved away from the end of the fabric if a guide is not required.

Figure 3   Swing Guide.

This edge guide is used for stitching straight lines when quilting. Use the adjustable guide, which is added to the presser foot, as a marker to indicate the distance to be maintained between the seams.

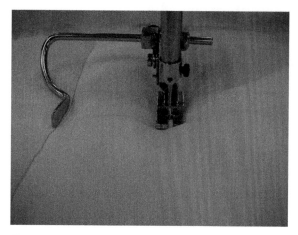

Figure 4   Edge Guide.

PRESSER FOOT

The standard **presser foot** can be replaced with a **compensating presser foot**, which also performs the function of edge guiding. The toes on a standard presser foot are fixed, while on a compensating foot the toes move up and down on springs. This foot is used where topstitching on a seam is required and there is a difference in height between the left and right side of the seam. On a seam of this nature, the presser foot toe at the lower level glides along the edge of the seam ridge and a line of stitching that is parallel with the ridge is achieved. This presser foot is used for topstitching on raised seams, attaching patch pockets, and so on.

Compensating presser feet are available in a variety of different widths.

Figure 5   Used for stitching 1mm from the edge.

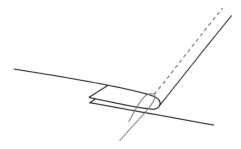

Figure 6

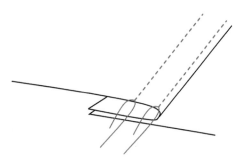

Figure 7   Used for stitching 5mm from the edge.   **Figure 8**

HEMMING FOOT

The folding device on the hemming foot controls and folds the edge of the fabric and presents the folded fabric to the needle point for stitching.

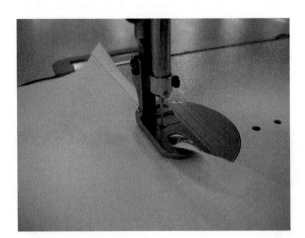

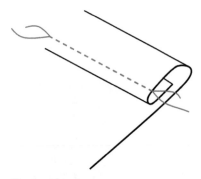

Figure 9   Hem Foot.   **Figure 10**

This type of folder is used for hemming scarves and shirts or hemming any part of a garment made from medium to lightweight fabric.

Hemming feet are available in several types, performing either a single or double turn hem in a variety of widths from 1mm to 4mm.

Figure 11

ZIPPER FOOT

There are a variety of types of zipper feet.

An invisible zip is inserted using the presser foot shown below. The teeth on an invisible zip are turned inwards and they join together on the inside of the garment. The teeth of the zip fit into the grooves in the presser foot and the specialised design of the foot enables the stitching to get close to the teeth of the zip.

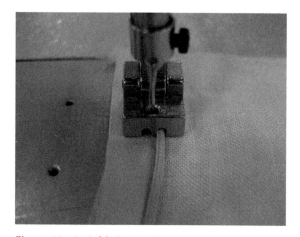

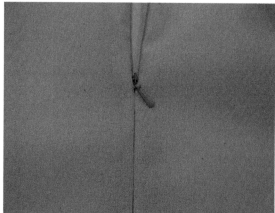

Figure 12   Invisible Presser Foot.

When attaching accessories such as piping onto a garment, a presser foot with a single toe enables stitching to get close to the piping, or this presser foot can be used when inserting a concealed or standard zip, enabling the stitching to get close to the zip teeth. See Chapter 8 for details of how to insert a concealed or standard zip.

Figure 13   Single Toe Presser Foot.

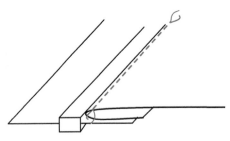

Figure 14

FOLDERS

Many folding attachments are available, from a binder for attaching a strip of binding or braid onto the edge of fabric such as an armhole or neckline, to a folder that will turn in the fabric's raw edges to create a lapped felled seam. See Chapter 2 for details of how to construct a lapped felled seam.

Figure 15   Folder for attaching binding.

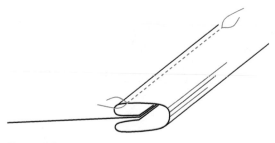

Figure 16

CHAPTER 4
NEEDLES & THREAD

The sewing machine needle, despite its low cost, is one of the most important components used when sewing. It performs the vital function of transporting the sewing thread to the sewing machine mechanism to form the stitches and protects the sewing thread during its passage through the fabric with minimum distortion to the fabric. Industrial sewing machines are capable of exceeding speeds of 6000 stitches per minute. When stitching closely woven fabric at this speed, the action of the needle generates friction and the needle can reach temperatures of 400 degrees centigrade. Not only does the temperature damage the fabric, but the hardness of the needle can be affected. Natural fabrics such as cotton can withstand high temperatures without much damage but a resin finish coating on a fabric or synthetic fabric, such as nylon, will melt.

PARTS OF THE NEEDLE

Needles are available in a range of sizes with several types of point and the choice of size and point type is determined by the fabric to be sewn.

The three categories are as follows.

Set Points

Within this category is the **set cloth point** used for sewing woven fabrics; the point is slightly rounded which displaces the yarns of the material being sewn without damaging them.

The **slim set point** is an acute point which is used in the Single Thread Chainstitch Blind stitch (103) machine for hemming fine to densely woven fabrics.

The **heavy set point** or stub point is used in button sewing machines. The blunt point will safely deflect the button into the correct position to enable the needle to pass through the holes in the button.

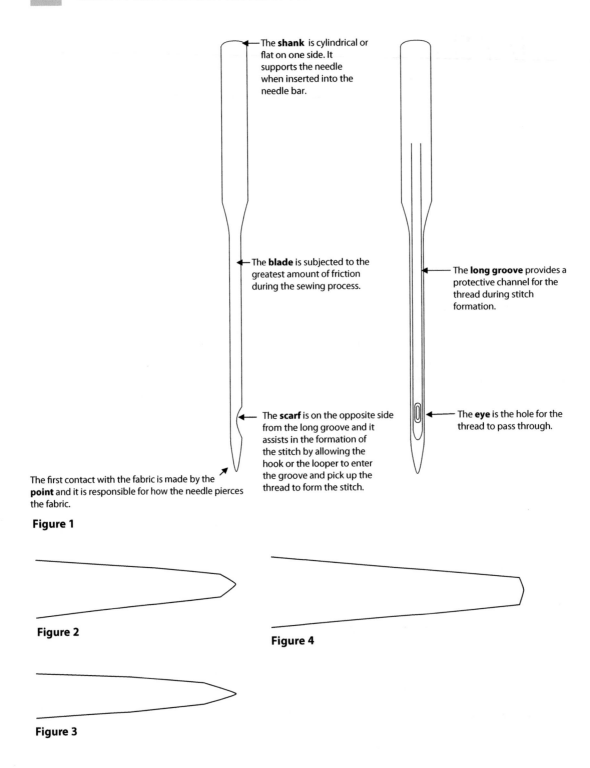

The **shank** is cylindrical or flat on one side. It supports the needle when inserted into the needle bar.

The **blade** is subjected to the greatest amount of friction during the sewing process.

The **long groove** provides a protective channel for the thread during stitch formation.

The **scarf** is on the opposite side from the long groove and it assists in the formation of the stitch by allowing the hook or the looper to enter the groove and pick up the thread to form the stitch.

The **eye** is the hole for the thread to pass through.

The first contact with the fabric is made by the **point** and it is responsible for how the needle pierces the fabric.

Figure 1

Figure 2

Figure 4

Figure 3

Ball points are available in three weights, light, medium and heavy, and are used for sewing knitted fabrics. Ball point needles do not pierce the threads of the fabric but displace the yarns in the fabric. The needle pushes between the fabric yarns rather than cutting or piercing the fabric.

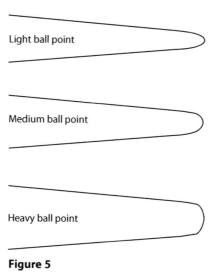

Light ball point

Medium ball point

Heavy ball point

Figure 5

Light ball points are used for sewing lightweight knitted fabrics. Medium and heavy ball points are used for sewing elastic fabrics containing rubber or elastomeric yarns; this needle point does not perforate the elastic yarns but pushes them aside.

Cutting Points

This category of needle is used for sewing leather and coated or laminated fabrics. These are classified and named according to the position of the cutting edge and its shape. The shape of this needle will create a slit (rather than a large hole) through which the thread will pass.

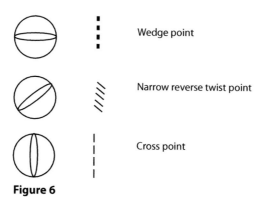

Wedge point

Narrow reverse twist point

Cross point

Figure 6

The fabric weight determines the size of the needle and thread to be used. When sewing fine fabrics both the needle and thread should be small in diameter. There are two needle sizing systems: the Number Metric and Singer system.

Needles are commonly labelled with two measurements separated by a slash. The Number Metric system simply gives the diameter of the needle in millimetres multiplied by 100; for example, a standard '80' needle is 80mm in diameter. The second number refers to the Singer system; for example, an 80/12 needle is simply the same needle measured by the two different systems.

The table below is a guide indicating the needle size and the stitch length for sewing a range of fabrics:

Table 1

FABRIC	NEEDLE SIZE	STITCH LENGTH
Lightweight: Chiffon, organza, crepe de chine, fine lace, lawn, voile, etc.	70/10	1 to 1.5mm
Mediumweight: Linen, poplin, drill, velveteen, needle-cord, taffeta, fine denim, tweed, etc.	80/12	1.5 to 2mm
Heavyweight: Terry towelling, denim, double-faced wool, gabardine, wide-wale corduroy	90/14	2 to 2.5mm

THREAD

Choosing the correct thread is fundamental; perfectly matched threads are often inconspicuous in a seam and, as a result, too little attention is paid to the choice of thread. The cost of thread contributes only a small fraction to the overall cost of the garment, but if a poor sewing thread is selected it can increase production costs significantly owing to frequent thread breaks.

When selecting the correct thread consider the following:

⇒ colour
⇒ size
⇒ construction
⇒ fibre contents
⇒ performance of the thread during the sewing process
⇒ performance of the thread in the completed garment during its lifetime in wear and cleaning
⇒ thread package.

Like other textile materials, sewing thread can be made up from different fibre types, constructions and finishes and each can influence the appearance and performance of the seam. Many thread sizes (thicknesses) are available and the choice of size is determined by the requirements of the fabric and product, which, in turn, determine the size of the sewing needle; for example, a blouse made from a fine satin fabric will be sewn with a fine thread, 180 thread and a 70/10 size needle. A leather bag will be sewn with a heavy, strong thread, 75 thread and a 90/14 size needle.

Threads from natural fibres include **silk threads** spun from a continuous filament or broken filament. This thread is strong with a lustrous appearance and it performs well in the sewing machine but it is costly. The high cost restricts its use to sewing buttonholes and topstitching on bespoke tailoring, haute couture garments and specialised embroidery.

Linen threads are spun from flax that produces an extremely strong thread used for stitching footwear, leather products and attaching buttons. Linen threads have been largely superseded by synthetic threads, which are also extremely strong.

Cotton is also constructed by spinning the longest cotton fibres. It has good sewing performance but the strength and abrasion resistance are inferior to synthetic threads. Cotton threads can also shrink when wet, causing pucker. Cotton threads are generally less affected by needle heat.

Threads from synthetic fibres are popular today; they do not rot and they have greater strength for their size with low shrinkage.

Polyester and Polyamide (nylon 66) are both formed by melting chips of polymer and extruding the molten polymer through a spinnerette, which is then cooled and collected to form yarn. The yarns are then stretched and crimped to produce a better frictional surface and either cut or stretched to produce lengths of fibre, which are spun into thread.

Thread made from spun yarns generally has:

⇒ Good sewing performance.
⇒ Good dimensional stability.
⇒ Good stitch locking properties in the seams because of the fibrous surfaces.
⇒ Abrasion resistance depending on the fibre.

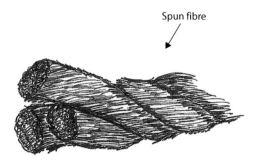

Spun fibre

Figure 7   Staple spun.

Alternatively, continuous multifilament yarns go through a process of imparting texture to the yarn which gives it a softness and bulk; this thread is commonly known as bulked thread. It is used extensively in the loopers **only** of Overedge, Multi-thread Chainstitch and Covering Chainstitch machines, as it gives a soft handle or feel to the seam with maximum seam coverage.

Viscose is used for embroidery only. Viscose threads have poor strength and durability.

Corespun thread has a continuous filament core wrapped with a sheath of spun fibre. The continuous filament synthetic core is strong and the spun fibre on the outside enhances the sewing properties. Corespun thread is strong but fine with good stretch properties and low shrinkage. Corespun threads enable adequate seam strength with finer thread, which means a finer size needle can be used.

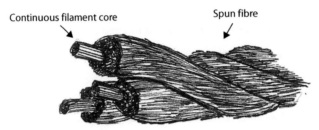

Continuous filament core   Spun fibre

Figure 8   Corespun.

THREAD CONSUMPTION

Measure the seam lengths in the garment and equate them to the stitch consumption rates below:

Table 2

STITCH TYPE	THREAD USAGE, IN CM, PER CM OF SEAM LENGTH
101 Single Thread Chainstitch	4
103 Single Thread Blind Stitch	4.5
301 Lockstitch	2.5
304 Zig Zag	5.5
401 Two Thread Chainstitch	5.5
406 Two Needle Chainstitch Bottom Cover	15.5

Table 2 *(continued)*

STITCH TYPE	THREAD USAGE, IN CM, PER CM OF SEAM LENGTH
407 Three Needle Chainstitch Bottom Cover	20
504 Three Thread Overedge	14
514 Four Thread Overedge	20
516 or 401.504 frequently called Five Thread Safety Stitch	20
602 Two Needle Cover Chainstitch frequently called Two Needle Flatlock	20
605 Three Needle Cover Chainstitch frequently called Three Needle Flatlock	27

THREAD SIZING

There are a number of systems used for indicating thread size: the Metric Count, Cotton Count and Denier Systems use ticket numbering systems to give an easy approximation of the specific size of the finished thread. The Metric Ticket Number system is the most common sizing system used universally. All thread sizing systems are based on length and weight, the general rule being the higher the thread number, the finer the thread, the lower the ticket number, the thicker the thread. The table below indicates the thread size to be used for particular applications.

Table 3

METRIC TICKET NO. (THREAD SIZE)	USED FOR:
120	General seaming for medium to light clothing, such as blouses, dresses, knitwear, skirts and trousers
180	Neatening and general seaming of lingerie, shirts and blouses made from lightweight fabrics
75	General seaming in work wear, jeans, gloves Decorative stitching Sewing buttons and buttonholing
40	Very heavy duty seaming, shoe bags Also used for decorative stitching, button sewing and buttonholing

Thread is available in different packages. **Spools** carry short lengths of 100 to 500 metres of thread and are used mainly in domestic sewing.

Cops carry 1000 to 2500 metres.

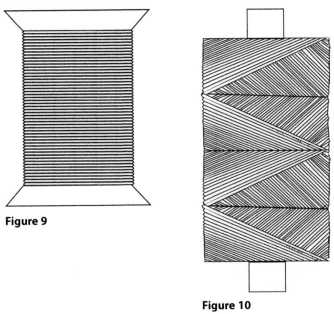

Figure 9

Figure 10

Cones carry 2500 to 5000 metres of thread and are the most economical to use in situations where thread consumption is high.

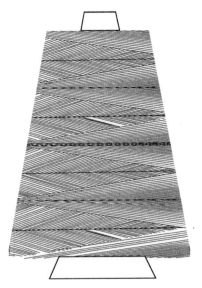

Figure 11

Vicones hold polished and continuous filament threads. The raised flange at the bottom is designed to prevent the thread from slipping off at the bottom.

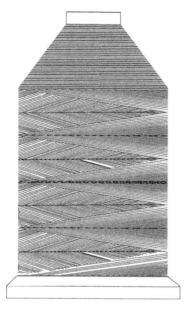

Figure 12

CHAPTER 5
INTERLINING

Interlinings are used to support, reinforce and control areas of garments such as collars, hems, facings and the fronts of jackets and coats. They can be sewn into the garment or attached by fusing.

The process of sewing in an interlining to a garment such as a tailored jacket is time consuming and requires a great deal of skill and therefore is mainly used in the production of bespoke tailored garments.

The alternative process is fusing, where interlining is bonded to the outer fabric by a thermoplastic resin.

Interlinings are available in a wide variety of weights and constructions such as woven, knitted or non-woven. Interlining should match the properties of the garment fabrics it will support in terms of weight and stability. For example, woven or non-woven interlining should be fused to the collar of a shirt made from woven poplin and a knitted interlining should be fused to the button stand of a t-shirt made from a knitted jersey fabric.

The interlining base cloth has a thermoplastic resin on the surface which is used to bond the base cloth to the garment part. The fusible interlining is laid on top of the fabric, heat is applied until it reaches the correct temperature and the two plies are pressed together and thereafter, handled as one. This process is often called laminating. It requires little skill and is not a time-consuming process but gives a consistent appearance.

Ways of applying resin to the base fabric are:

⇒ **Scatter coated:** Irregularly shaped resin dots are applied in random quantities to the base cloth. Generally, this type of fusible is used where a uniform handle is not critical.
⇒ **Dry dot printed:** Resin is deposited onto the fabric in a regular, controlled pattern by means of a screen or engraved roller. This type of fusible is generally used on men's suits and coat fronts. It will give a good, uniform and natural handle. The dots on the fusible can vary from 3 to 12 per square cm.

⇒ **Paste coated:** The resin is applied to the base cloth in an even, all-over layer. This will give a very firm handle and is generally used on shirt collars and cuffs.

Heat, pressure and **time** are the three essential factors required to fuse interlining onto the garment parts. Correct and controlled amounts of each are required.

⇒ The temperature should be high enough to melt the resin.
⇒ Enough consistent pressure should be applied to get a good contact between the fabric and even penetration of the resin onto the outer fabric.
⇒ Sufficient fusing time is needed to reach the correct temperature and allow the resin to flow onto the fabric.

FUSING EQUIPMENT

A number of different types of fusing equipment have been developed, providing controlled heat and pressure conditions, such as the flat bed fusing press below, where the garment parts with the interlining placed on top are positioned on the bottom plate and the top plate sandwiches the garment parts and interlining. With controlled heat and temperature, the two garment pieces are laminated together.

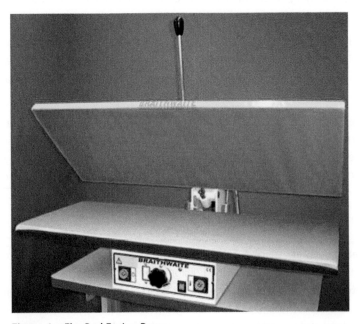

Figure 1   Flat Bed Fusing Press.

In the continuous fusing press, a conveyor belt transports the garment parts with the interlining placed on top to a heated chamber, pressure is applied for a controlled time and the conveyor belt then transports the garment parts to the cooling station.

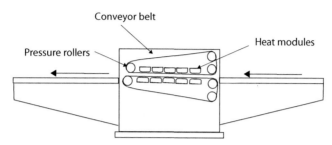

Figure 2   Continuous Fusing Press.

APPLYING INTERLINING

Interlining patterns should not include seam allowances. Interlining should be applied to the garment parts coloured yellow in the following garment types.

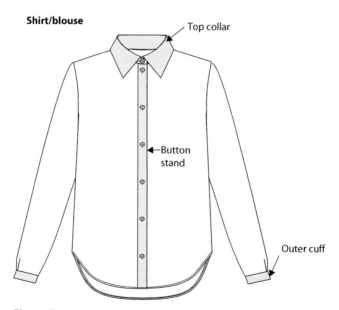

Figure 3

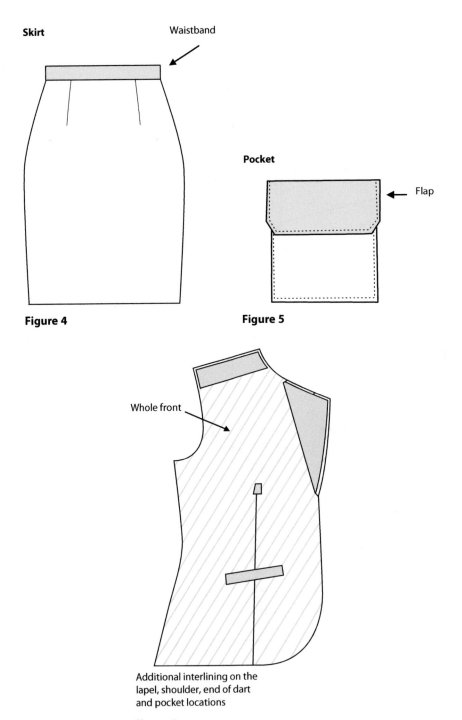

Skirt

Waistband

Figure 4

Pocket

Flap

Figure 5

Whole front

Additional interlining on the
lapel, shoulder, end of dart
and pocket locations

Figure 6

Tailored jacket

Collar

Facing

Two Piece Sleeve

Sleeve crown,
underarm and cuff

Back

Back neck, shoulder
and underarm

Vent

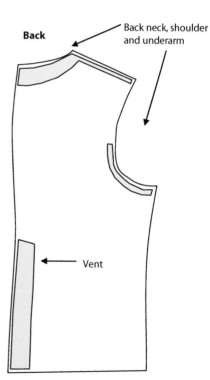

Figure 7

CHAPTER 6
SEWING DARTS

Darts are present on items of clothing such as skirts, trousers, dresses and jackets. They are the simplest way of providing suppression within a garment. A dart reduces excess fabric to create shape and contour in a garment made from woven fabrics. Knitted fabrics stretch and mould around the shape of the body but woven fabrics have limited stretch characteristics. When creating a close-fitting garment using woven fabrics, the insertion of darts will suppress the waist area and bestow fullness to areas of the garment such as the bust and hips.

Single ended darts are used in skirts and trousers to suppress the waist area and provide shape to accommodate the hip and tummy areas. A single ended dart is also used when constructing close-fitted upper torso garments; the dart will suppress the waist area of the garment and provide shape for the bust.

This type of dart should be stitched from the widest end to the point of the dart. A curved, not a straight, line of stitching is used to ensure that the contour of the dart matches with the body shape.

Notches on the edge of the fabric will mark the dart location. Fold the fabric and align the notches, then using the Lockstitch (301) back-tack at the start and stitch in a slight curve as shown in Figure 2. Continue stitching 1cm below the end of the dart, run off the fabric and form an approximate 1cm chain of stitches to secure the end of the dart.

Double ended darts are usually found on dresses and jackets.

This type of dart should be stitched from the point to point using a curved line of stitching, not a straight line, as shown in Figure 4.

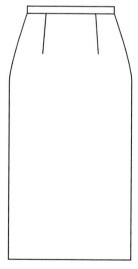

Figure 1

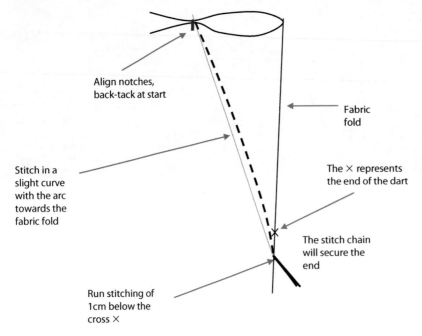

Align notches,
back-tack at start

Fabric
fold

Stitch in a
slight curve
with the arc
towards the
fabric fold

The × represents
the end of the dart

The stitch chain
will secure the
end

Run stitching of
1cm below the
cross ×

Figure 2

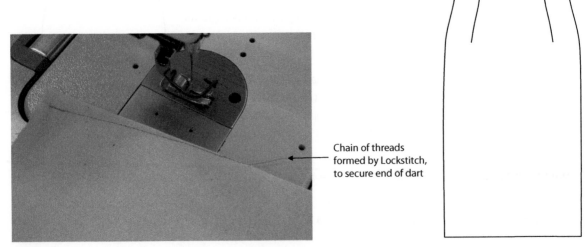

Figure 3

Chain of threads
formed by Lockstitch,
to secure end of dart

Figure 4

Crosses or spots are usually used to mark the dart location. Fold the fabric on the top dart point through to the bottom dart point and align the two middle points.

Using the Lockstitch (301) back-tack at the start and stitch in a slight curve as shown in Figure 6. Continue stitching 1cm below the end of the dart, run off the fabric and form an approximate 1cm chain of stitches to secure the end of the dart.

Figure 5

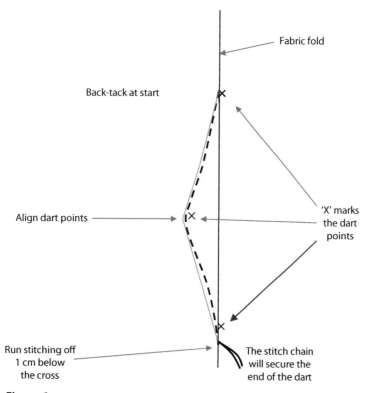

Fabric fold

Back-tack at start

Align dart points

'X' marks the dart points

Run stitching off 1 cm below the cross

The stitch chain will secure the end of the dart

Figure 6

A demonstration of sewing single ended and double ended darts can be viewed online at www .wiley.com.

CHAPTER 7
FRONT EDGE FASTENINGS

There are a variety of front opening constructions for finishing the edge of a shirt, blouse or a garment with a button-through opening.

Each of the front edges covered has a different construction, however the finished appearance may look similar; for example, the finished appearance of the traditional strap/placket and the grown-on front edge look similar but they are constructed differently.

As illustrated in Figure 1, the front where the buttons are applied has a simpler construction than the front edge with buttonholes. The front where the buttons are located is usually plain and simple to construct as it is hidden by the front edge with the buttonholes. This edge is frequently referred to as a 'strap' or 'placket'.

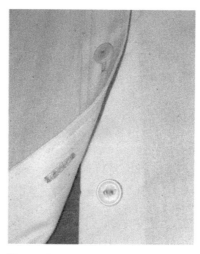

Figure 1

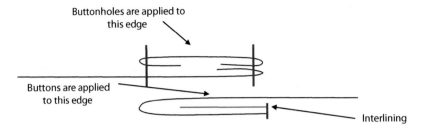

Buttonholes are applied to this edge

Buttons are applied to this edge

Interlining

Figure 2 Simplified seam diagram.

The plain front edge is a simple, non-bulky construction and is frequently used only on the side with the buttons attached. One of the following more decorative finishes will be used on the side with the buttonholes.

For a plain, simple appearance, use this front edge on both sides of the garment.

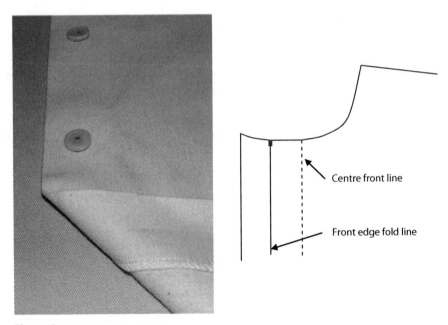

Centre front line

Front edge fold line

Figure 3

1. If the fabric is lightweight, an interlining is needed to reduce the strain that the buttons can put on this edge. This is attached when the edge is neatened using the Three Thread Overedge stitch (504).
2. Fold back the facing at the notch and press.

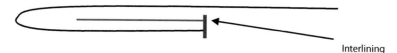

Interlining

Figure 4   Simplified seam diagram.

The traditional strap/placket has an additional strip of fabric (known as a strap or placket) attached. This finish is attached to the side of the garment where the buttonholes are inserted.

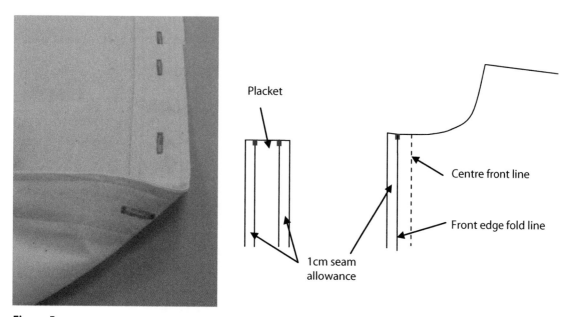

Placket

Centre front line

Front edge fold line

1cm seam allowance

Figure 5

1. Place the right side of the placket to the wrong side of the garment front and attach the placket using the Lockstitch (301).

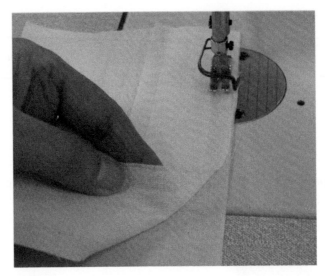

Figure 6

2. Fold the placket into position at the notches and press.
3. With the right side of the placket uppermost, apply two rows of topstitching.

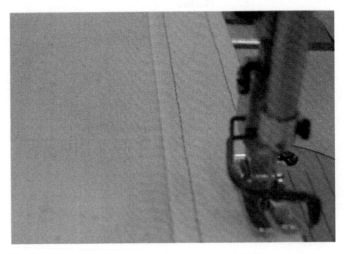

Figure 7

4. The buttonholes are then inserted.

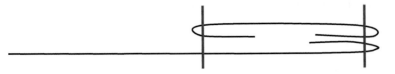

Figure 8 Simplified seam diagram.

The grown-on front edge has sufficient fabric to form the button placket and is added to the front of the garment where the buttonholes are inserted.

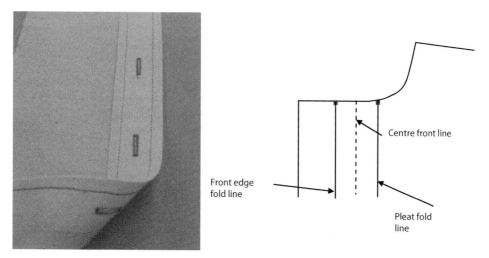

Figure 9

1. The folds in the grown-on front edge are indicated with notches. Fold the fabric at the notches and stitch the first row of stitching using the Lockstitch (301). This row of stitching will form a pleat. See Figure 10, Stage One.

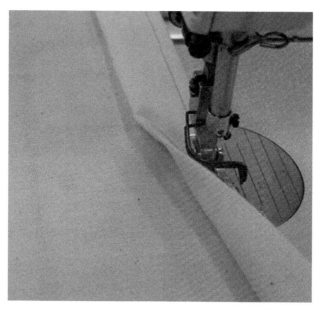

Figure 10

2.   Fold the placket into position and press.

3.   With the right side of the placket uppermost, apply topstitching, see Figure 11, Stage Two.

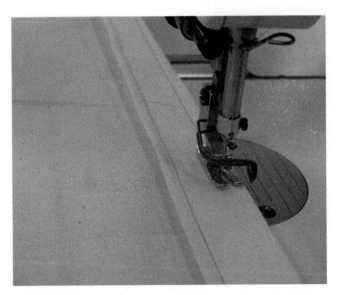

Figure 11

4.   The buttonholes are then inserted.

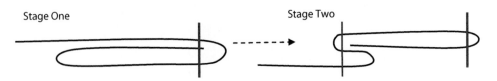

Stage One   Stage Two

Figure 12

The concealed front edge is frequently known as a fly front. On the edge where the buttonholes are inserted, additional fabric is added to form the button placket.

This additional flap of fabric covers the buttonholes.

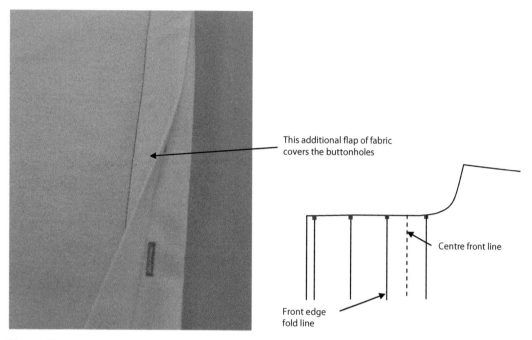

This additional flap of fabric covers the buttonholes

Centre front line

Front edge fold line

Figure 13

1. The folds in the concealed front edge are indicated with notches. Fold the fabric at the notches and stitch one row of stitching using the Lockstitch (301). See Figure 14, Stage One.

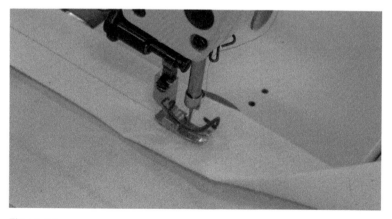

Figure 14

2.   Press into position and insert the buttonholes.

Figure 15

A demonstration of sewing front edges can be viewed online at www.wiley.com.

CHAPTER 8
INSERTING ZIP FASTENINGS

There are many zip types – invisible, open-ended and closed-ended – and they can be inserted into garments in a number of ways depending on the style and the function of the garment. A zip has two strips of fabric tape that link together with specially shaped teeth made from metal, plastic, polyester or nylon.

Figure 1

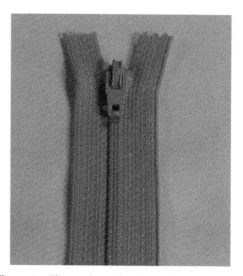

Figure 2 The teeth can be made from a **continuous coil** of polyester monofilament with a slider that, when moved, links or unlinks the teeth.

Figure 3 **Profile moulded** individual teeth made from plastic which couple together. This type of zip has a decorative appearance and is used extensively in casual and sportswear garments.

Zips with teeth made from metal, usually brass, are traditionally used in jeans or work wear garments.

INVISIBLE ZIP INSERTION

The teeth on an invisible zip are different from those on a conventional zip, as they are turned onto the inside so that they do not show, giving the impression of being concealed in the seam, as seen below.

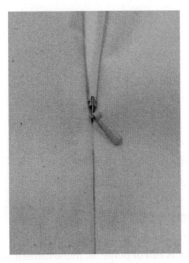

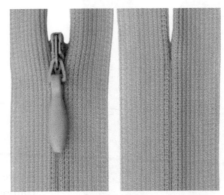

Figure 4 An invisible zip inserted into a garment.

Figure 5 An invisible zip.

Figure 6 Invisible zip, simplified seam diagram.

Due to the invisible zip being sewn to a single thickness of fabric rather than being sewn underneath a folded edge of fabric, it takes much less skill to attach an invisible zip than any other type.

The seam is closed afterwards, using a half presser foot to enable the stitches to get as close as possible to the zip stitching.

Figure 7 When inserting an invisible zip, the presser foot shown is used to enable the stitching to be located close to the teeth of the zip. The zip is attached to the garment before the seam is joined and it is attached with the zip itself fully open.

1. Use the Three Thread Overedge stitch (504) to neaten the seam edges of the seam where the zip is going to be inserted.
2. Attach the invisible zipper presser foot to the Lockstitch (301) sewing machine. The presser foot for inserting an invisible zip can be seen in Figure 7.
3. Identify the right side of the zip. (The teeth do not show on the right side.) Open the zip and place the right side of the zip tape to the right side of the garment. The top of the zip should align with the top edge of the fabric (see Figure 8).

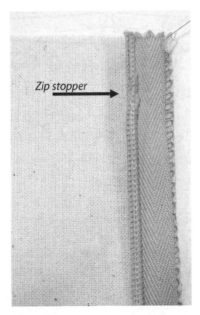

Figure 8

4. Insert the teeth into the groove in the presser foot and stitch each side of the zip to the garment, back-tacking at the beginning of the seam.

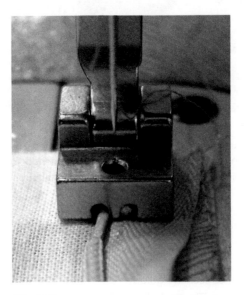

Figure 9

5. When sewing the tape onto the garment, use your finger to uncurl the zip teeth, this will facilitate the needle getting closer to the zip teeth (see Figure 10).

Figure 10

6. Stitch to the zip slider and back-tack to secure the end of the seam.

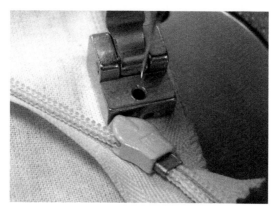

Figure 11

7. Now, attach the other side of the zip, but insert the teeth into the other groove in the presser foot.
8. To close the seam, attach a half presser foot (with one toe); this presser foot will enable the stitching to join up and get close to the zip stitching (see Figure 12).

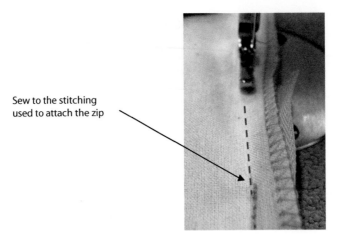

Sew to the stitching used to attach the zip

Figure 12

9. Finally, secure the tape at the bottom of the zip tape to the seam allowances using the Lockstitch (301).

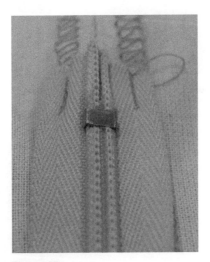

Figure 13

CONCEALED OR STANDARD ZIP WITH GUARD INSERTION

This type of zip insertion is commonly used on womenswear, skirts, dresses, etc. The standard zip is as illustrated in Figures 14 and 15 of this chapter and the edge of the fabric folds over the zip teeth and tape and conceals the zip in the seam. A guard, as shown in Figure 15, is attached under the zip and prevents the zip teeth from catching on the wearer's underclothing when opening or closing the zip. A zip guard is rectangular in shape and it is usually cut from the same fabric as the garment.

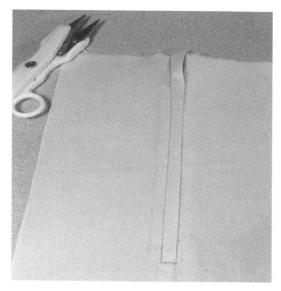

Figure 14

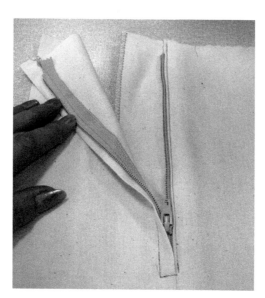

Figure 15

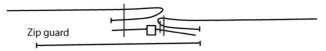

Zip guard

Figure 16   Concealed or standard zip with guard insertion, simplified seam diagram.

1. Use the Three Thread Overedge stitch (504) to neaten the seam edges of the seam where the zip is going to be inserted and three sides of the zip guard.

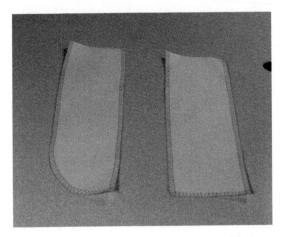

Figure 17

2. Use the Lockstitch (301) to close the seam using a 1.5cm seam allowance, but leave an opening to insert the zip and attach the half presser foot with one toe.

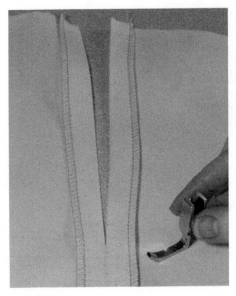

Figure 18

3. Place the right side of the zip to the right side of the fabric and attach the zip tape using the Lockstitch (301).

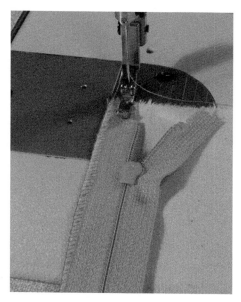

Figure 19   The 'single toe' zipper presser foot will allow the stitching to get close to the teeth of the zip.

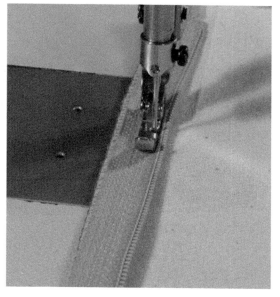

Figure 20

4. Place the zip guard at the back of the zip, aligning the edge of the zip guard with the edge of the zip tape and with the right side of the garment up, attach the zip guard (see Figures 21 and 22).

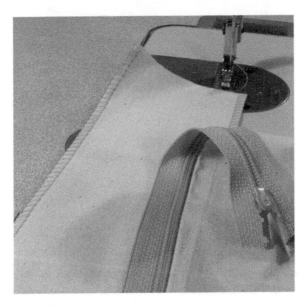

Figure 21

Figure 22

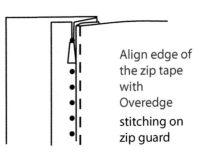

Align edge of the zip tape with Overedge stitching on zip guard

Figure 23

5. Fold the zip guard back and pin it, to prevent it from getting caught in this next row of stitching. Continuing to work on the right side of the garment, fold the seam allowance on the other side, moving it over to overlap the zip just enough to cover the zip teeth. Sew using the Lockstitch (301), backtacking at the beginning and end of the seam (see Figures 24 and 25).

Figure 24

Figure 25

6. Unpin the zip guard and flip it back into position. Finally, stitch across the bottom of the zip. This short row of stitching will also hold the zip guard in position.

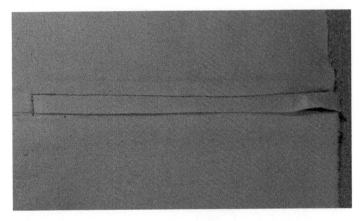

Figure 26

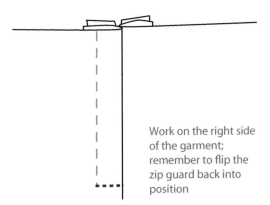

Work on the right side of the garment; remember to flip the zip guard back into position

Figure 27

A demonstration of inserting an invisible and concealed zip can be viewed online at www.wiley.com.

CHAPTER 9

ATTACHING WAISTBANDS

A variety of possible methods is available for finishing the waist edges of skirts and trousers. Which method is used on a particular garment depends on the appearance that is required and the fabric that the garment is made from.

In general, waistband constructions on men's trousers are more complicated than those on ladies' wear and children's wear and those on jeans.

If a skirt is lined, the lining is attached to the skirt before the waistband is attached.

This section covers the standard 'run on and close down' waistband, usually used on skirts and trousers made from woven fabric, and an elasticated waistband on a garment made from a knitted fabric.

STANDARD 'RUN ON AND CLOSE DOWN' WAISTBAND APPLICATION

1. Apply fusible interlining onto the waistband; this will stabilise the waistband and prevent it from stretching. Using slotted waistband interlining will make it easier to fold the waistband into position (see Figure 2).

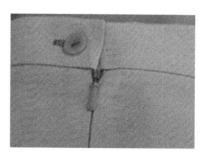

Figure 1

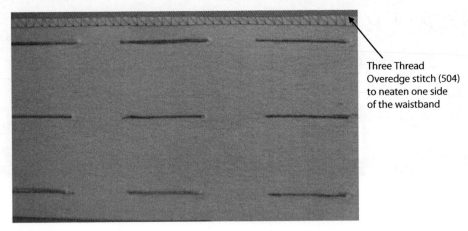

Three Thread
Overedge stitch (504)
to neaten one side
of the waistband

Figure 2

2. Use the Three Thread Overedge stitch (504) to neaten one side of the waistband.
3. Turn the garment through to the correct side, place the correct side of the waistband to the correct side of the garment and align the non-neatened edge of the waistband with the waist of the garment, leaving approximately 1cm protruding beyond the zip guard. Using the Lockstitch (301), sew in the slots attaching the waistband onto the garment, back-tacking at the beginning and end of the seam (see Figure 3).

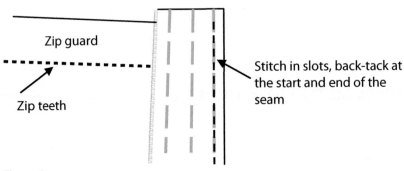

Zip guard

Zip teeth

Stitch in slots, back-tack at the start and end of the seam

Figure 3

4. Fold the waistband ends, as illustrated below.

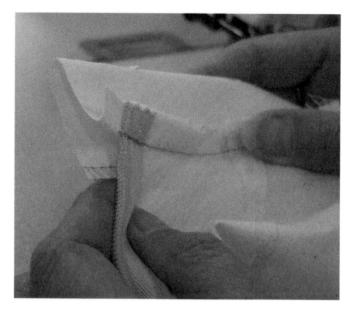

Figure 4

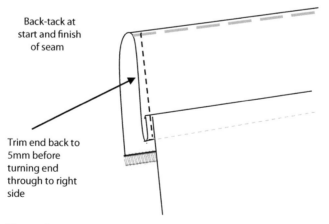

Back-tack at
start and finish
of seam

Trim end back to
5mm before
turning end
through to right
side

Figure 5

Stitch approximately 2mm away from the finished edges of the garment (see Figure 6).

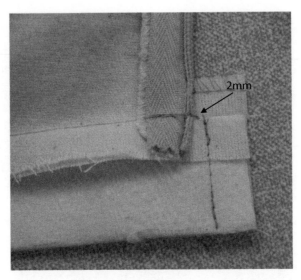

Figure 6

5. Turn waistband end through to the correct side, ensuring that the corner is fully pushed out. Use scissors to assist with this task, taking care not to apply too great a pressure, as the point of the object could pierce the end of the waistband.

6. If the zip does not have a zip guard attached, bag out the other end of the waistband to form an extension for the button and turn through to the right side. See Figure 7 below.

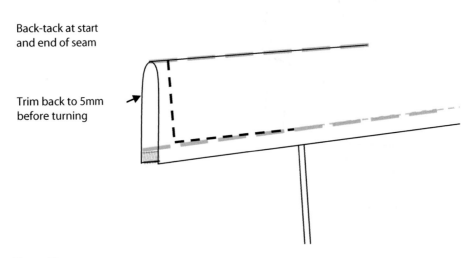

Figure 7

7. Fold the waistband into position. All raw edges should be enclosed within the waistband and the Overedge neatened edge of the waistband should hang down.

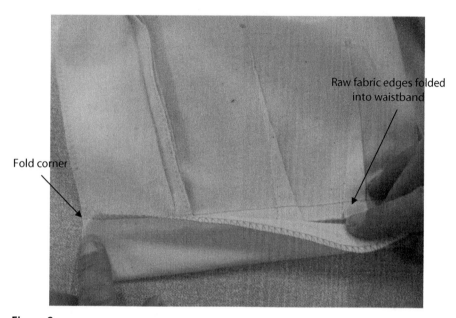

Fold corner

Raw fabric edges folded into waistband

Figure 8

Skirt

Figure 9 Simplified seam diagram.

8. Starting at the extension end and working on the correct side of the garment, use the Lockstitch (301) to sink stitch the waistband down.

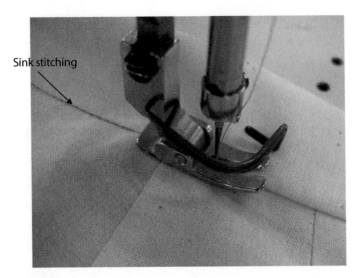

Sink stitching

Figure 10

9. Insert the buttonhole on the front of the waistband, fasten the zip and mark the button position on the button extension. Finally, sew on the button.

ELASTICATED WAISTBAND

This type of waistband is frequently applied to skirts, trousers or leggings made from knitted fabrics with good stretch characteristics. These garments can be pulled over the hips without the garment having an opening such as a zip.

The elastic can be simply secured into position at the side seams of the garment.

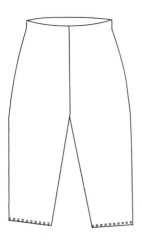

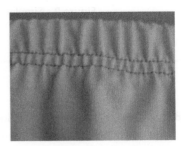

Figure 11

Or, the elastic can be fully secured in position with the Two Needle Chainstitch Bottom Cover (406):

1. Cut the elastic 10% shorter in length than the waist circumference, fold the elastic in half and mark the midpoint with chalk.

2. Using the Lockstitch (301), overlap and join the ends of the elastic to form a circle (see Figure 12).

Figure 12

The elastic can be attached to the garment directly using the Three Thread Overedge stitch (504), but this may prove to be difficult, therefore the elastic can be stitched onto the waist and secured in position using the Lockstitch (301) and then stitched with the Three Thread Overedge stitch (504). This will help to simplify the process.

3. Lay the elastic on the wrong side of the garment; place the overlap of elastic at the side seam. Use a 5mm seam allowance, stretch the elastic until the chalk mark aligns with the other side seam.

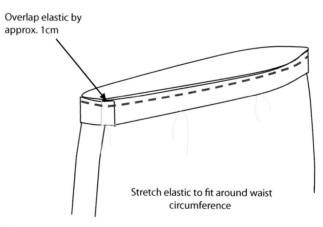

Overlap elastic by approx. 1cm

Stretch elastic to fit around waist circumference

Figure 13

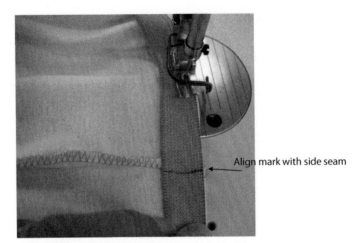

Align mark with side seam

Figure 14

4. Stitch around the waist circumference using the Three Thread Overedge stitch (504), taking care not to cut into the elastic.
5. Turn the garment to the right side and secure elastic in the downward position, use the Lockstitch (301) to sink stitch the elastic in position at the side seams (see Figure 15).
   Or, the elastic can be fully secured in position with the Two Needle Chainstitch Bottom Cover (406).

Work on the right side of the garment and secure the elastic in position at the side seams.

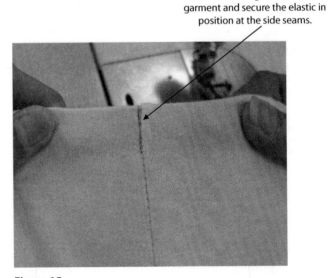

Figure 15

A demonstration of sewing waistbands can be viewed online at www.wiley.com.

CHAPTER 10

ASSEMBLING & ATTACHING POCKETS

The inclusion of a pocket can be for a number of reasons, such as to enable the wearer to carry essentials that they require or simply to create a style feature on the garment. There are many different types of pocket which can be classified into two general categories: a pocket that is sewn onto the garment, such as a patch pocket, or a pocket that is sewn into the garment, such as a slant pocket or a jetted pocket.

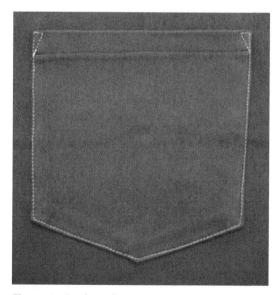

Figure 1   Patch pocket.

Figure 2   Slant pocket.

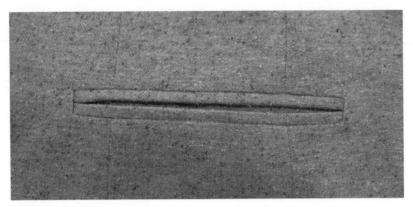

Figure 3   Jetted pocket.

PATCH POCKET

A patch pocket is one of the simplest pockets to construct. The size of the pocket should accommodate the hand. Decide on the pocket length and width by measuring the hand size.

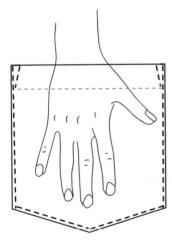

Figure 4

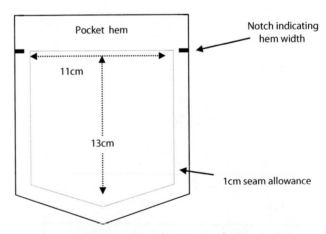

Figure 5   A simple patch pocket pattern shape.

Pocket hem

Notch indicating hem width

11cm

13cm

1cm seam allowance

1. Use the Three Thread Overedge stitch (504) to neaten the top edge of the pocket.

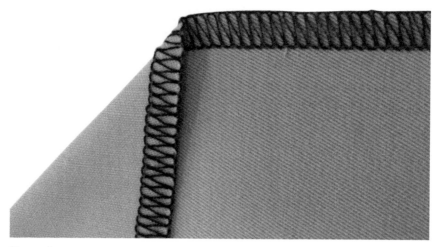

Figure 6

2. Fold over the hem of the pocket at the notches and use the Lockstitch (301) to sew (bag out) each corner by stitching 1cm from the edge.

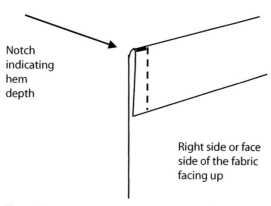

Notch indicating hem depth

Right side or face side of the fabric facing up

Figure 7

3. Trim surplus fabric from each pocket corner (see Figure 8).

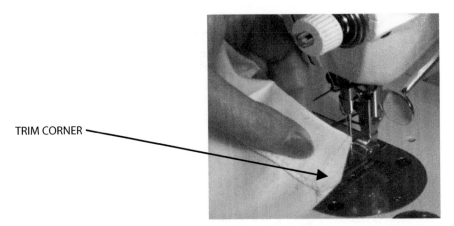

TRIM CORNER

Figure 8

4. Fold the pocket hem and, using an iron, fold the remaining raw edges around the template (see Figure 9).

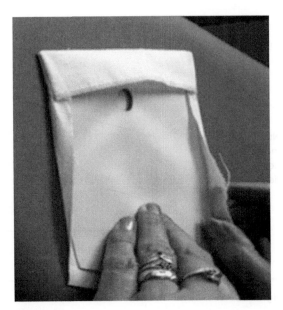

Figure 9

5. Using the Lockstitch (301), secure the hem in position by sewing on top of the Overedge stitch.
6. The pocket is now ready to attach to the garment.
   Using a Lockstitch (301), stitch the pocket onto the garment. The stitching line should be located 2mm from the folded fabric edge. Reinforce the weak points at each side of the pocket mouth.

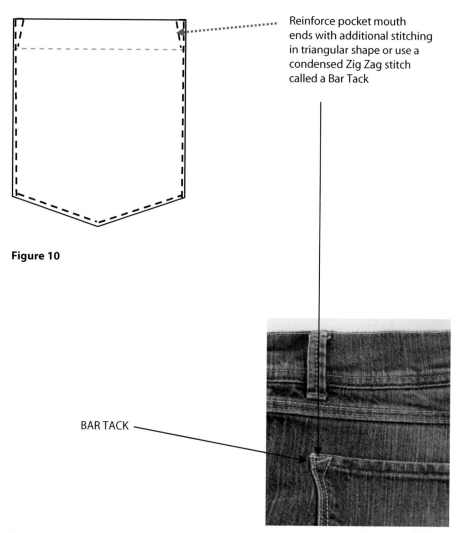

Reinforce pocket mouth ends with additional stitching in triangular shape or use a condensed Zig Zag stitch called a Bar Tack

Figure 10

BAR TACK

Figure 11

SHAPED POCKETS

This type of pocket is usually found on trousers and skirts. The pocket mouth shape is cut from the front of the garment and the pocket mouth can be straight, slanted or shaped.

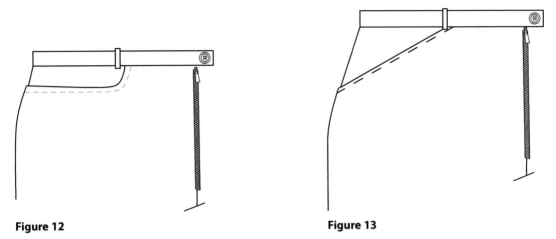

Figure 12

Figure 13

The slant pocket is assembled from the following pieces. The pocket mouth is determined by the width of your hand.

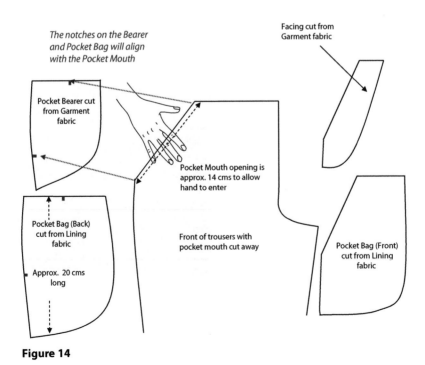

The notches on the Bearer and Pocket Bag will align with the Pocket Mouth

Facing cut from Garment fabric

Pocket Bearer cut from Garment fabric

Pocket Mouth opening is approx. 14 cms to allow hand to enter

Pocket Bag (Back) cut from Lining fabric

Approx. 20 cms long

Front of trousers with pocket mouth cut away

Pocket Bag (Front) cut from Lining fabric

Figure 14

The pocket mouth opening is created by removing a section from the garment and this gap is filled in by a pocket bearer. It is cut from the fabric that the garment is made from. The pocket bags (front and back) are usually cut from a thin fabric such as lining to reduce bulk when the pocket is sewn. The pocket facing is also cut from the garment fabric.

1. Use the Three Thread Overedge stitch (504) to neaten the curved bottom edge (shown in Figure 15) of the bearer and the facing.

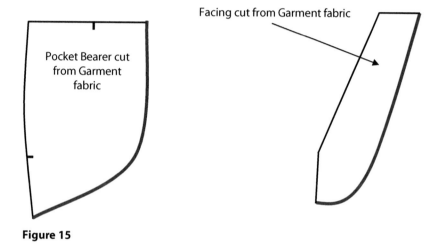

Figure 15

2. Position the bearer on top of the pocket bag (back), align the notches on the bearer with the pocket bag and use the Lockstitch (301) to sew the bearer to the back pocket bag by stitching on top of the Overedge stitch around the curved bottom edge (see Figure 16).

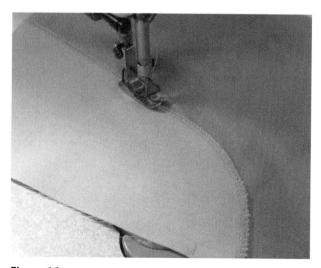

Figure 16

3. Position the facing on top of the pocket bag (front) and use the Lockstitch (301) to sew the facing to the front pocket bag by stitching on top of the Overedge stitch around the curved bottom edge (see Figure 17).

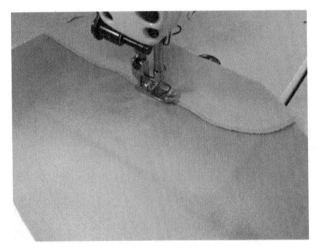

Figure 17

4. With a 5mm seam allowance, sew the pocket bag (front) to the garment using the Lockstitch (301), then **understitch** this seam also using the Lockstitch (301).

Figure 18

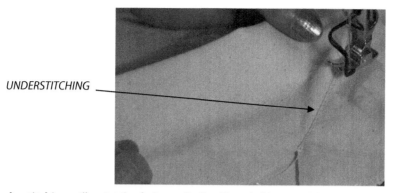

Figure 19   Understitching will assist the facing to lie flat. The stitching goes through the facing and the seam allowances of the facing and the garment to hold everything in place. Understitching does not show on the outside of the garment.

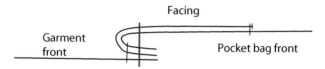

Figure 20   Simplified seam diagram.

5. Fold the pocket bag to the inside and now topstitch the pocket mouth, stitching 5mm from the edge.

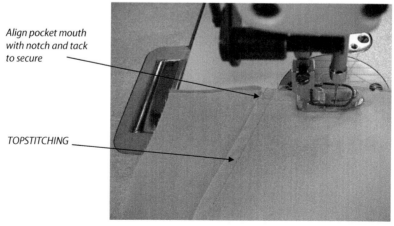

Figure 21

6. Align the pocket mouth with the notches on the bearer and secure the pocket mouth with the bearer by tacking using the Lockstitch (301) at the notch locations.

7. Finally, close the pocket bag by stitching around the curved edge of the pocket bag using the Five Thread Overedge (516). See Figure 22 below.

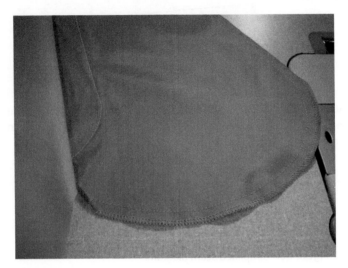

Figure 22

JETTED POCKET

Jetted, flap and welted pockets are usually associated with tailored garments such as jackets, coats and trousers. These three pockets are manufactured using the same basic construction principles, where the pocket opening or mouth is cut into the garment and the raw edges are subsequently neatened by the following:

⇒   Two additional narrow strips of fabric called jets are used when constructing the jetted pocket.

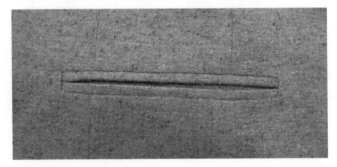

Figure 23   Jetted pocket.

⇒ One additional band of fabric known as a welt is applied when constructing the welt pocket.

Figure 24   Welt pocket.

⇒ A jet and an additional shaped piece of fabric known as a flap, which covers the pocket mouth, are applied when constructing the flap pocket.

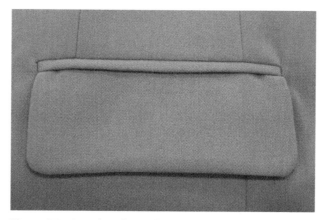

Figure 25   Jetted pocket with welt.

These pocket types can be located on a garment in a variety of positions, sometimes through darts and seams and at an angle that will facilitate easy access to the pocket for the wearer.

A jetted pocket is produced from the following pieces:

Two rectangular pieces called **jets**, with interlining fused onto the wrong side of the fabric. This will stabilise the jets, which form the pocket mouth from stretching.

One rectangular piece called a **blind**, usually cut from the same fabric type as the jets. This is the piece of fabric that is seen when the pocket mouth is open.

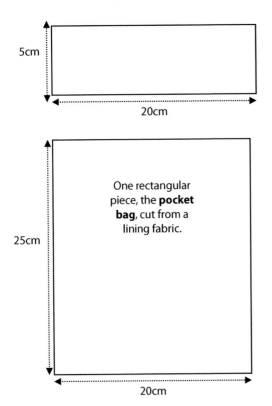

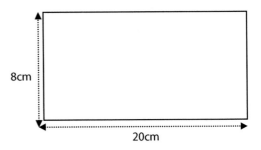

One rectangular piece, the **pocket bag**, cut from a lining fabric.

Figure 26   Suggested dimensions for jetted pocket for a tailored jacket.

Creating the Jets

1.   Using tailor's chalk, indicate the pocket mouth opening on the correct side of the garment.

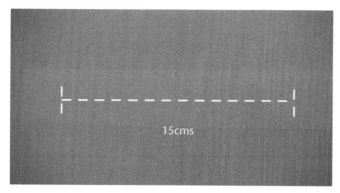

Figure 27   The width of the pocket mouth should be large enough to accommodate a hand.

Apply a rectangle of fusible interlining to the wrong side of the fabric directly behind the pocket mouth. The interlining will reinforce and stabilise the pocket mouth and prevent it from stretching during wear.

All seams in this pocket are stitched using a Lockstitch.

2. Position the edge of the first jet (correct side of the jet to correct side of the fabric) on the line and stitch using a 0.5cm seam width from the edge. Back-tack at the beginning and end of the seam.

3. Now, position the second jet by butting it close to the first jet edge and attach it in the same manner, ensuring that the lines of stitching are parallel (see Figure 28).

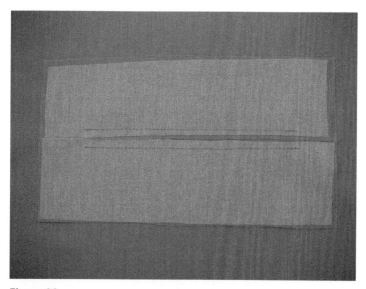

Figure 28

4. Using scissors, cut along the chalk line between the jets and mitre into the corners. Take care not to cut into the jets at this stage (see Figure 29).

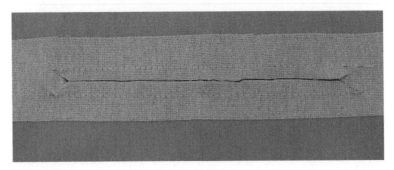

Figure 29

5. Turn the jets through to the wrong side of the garment and press the seams open, allowing one half of the seam to go down into the jet and the other half to go into the garment.
6. Secure the jets in position by stitching in the seam. This is called **sink stitching**. Back-tack at the beginning and end of the seams and ensure that the jets are equal in width (see Figure 30).

Sink stitching

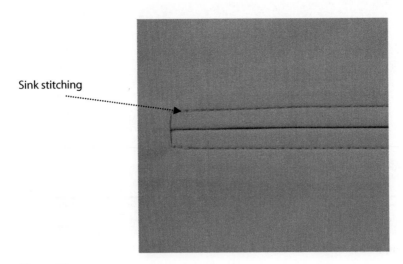

Figure 30

7. Turn to the inside of the garment and stitch to secure the mitres, frequently referred to as 'fish tails' (see Figure 31).

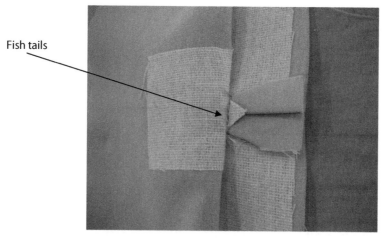

Fish tails

Figure 31

Attaching the Pocket Bag to the Jets

8. Attach the pocket bag to the bottom jet using a 1cm seam and then **understitch** to keep the seam flat (see Figure 32).

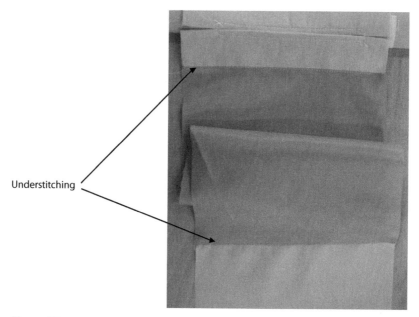

Understitching

Figure 32

Attach the blind to the other end of the pocket bag and again understitch to keep the seam flat.

9. Fold the blind and the pocket bag up to meet with the top jet. Attach a half presser foot to the sewing machine, which will allow closer access to the original stitching line used to secure the jet. Secure the top jet to the pocket bag by stitching on top of the original row of stitching.

10. Insert a pleat in the pocket bag by folding the fabric upwards; this pleat will prevent drag on the pocket mouth when it has objects in it. Stitch around the pocket bag (see Figure 33).

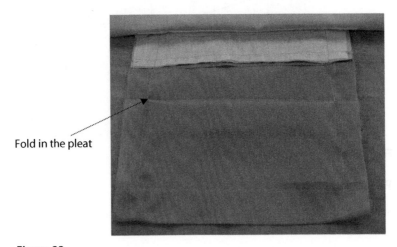

Fold in the pleat

Figure 33

WELT POCKET

A welt pocket is manufactured using similar construction principles to the jetted pocket.

The pocket can be positioned at an angle or straight on the garment.

A welt pocket is produced from the following pieces;

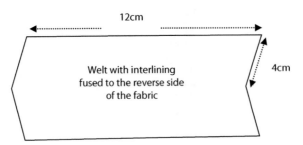

12cm

Welt with interlining
fused to the reverse side
of the fabric

4cm

Figure 34   Suggested dimensions for welt pocket for a tailored jacket.

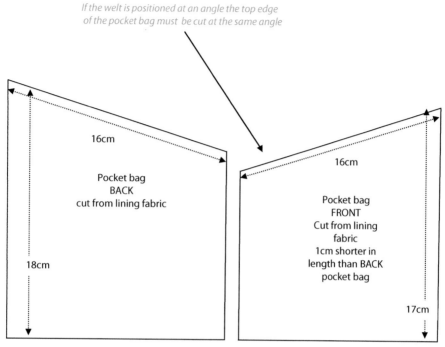

If the welt is positioned at an angle the top edge of the pocket bag must be cut at the same angle

16cm

Pocket bag
BACK
cut from lining fabric

18cm

16cm

Pocket bag
FRONT
Cut from lining
fabric
1cm shorter in
length than BACK
pocket bag

17cm

Figure 35   If the welt is positioned at an angle, the top edge of the pocket bag must be cut at the same angle.

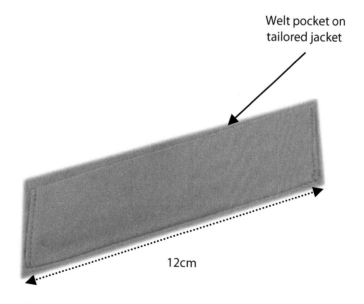

Welt pocket on
tailored jacket

12cm

Figure 36

1. With chalk, mark the pocket opening location on the front of the garment. This chalk line is 12cm long. Apply a rectangle of fusible interlining to the wrong side of the fabric directly behind the pocket mouth. The interlining will reinforce and stabilise the pocket mouth and prevent it from stretching during wear.

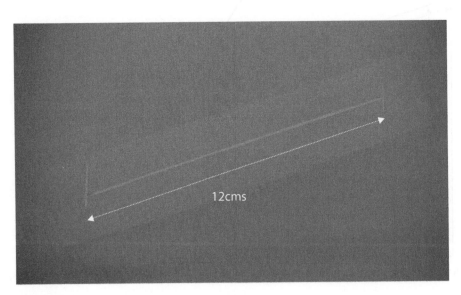

12cms

Figure 37

2. Fold the welt and use the Lockstitch (301) to close each end using a 5mm seam allowance. (Stitch with right sides of fabric together. Back-tack at the start and end of the seam.)

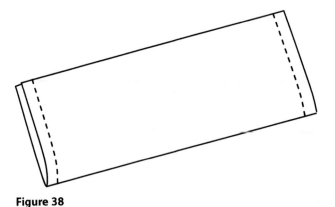

Figure 38

3. Turn welt through and press.
4. Place raw edge of welt on lower side of chalk line and attach welt to garment with a 5mm seam width using the Lockstitch (301). See Figure 31 below.

Align edge of Welt with chalk mark

Figure 39

5. Place the shortest pocket bag (FRONT) on top of the welt and sew using a 5mm seam along the length of the welt seam. Back-tack at the beginning and end of the line (see Figure 40).

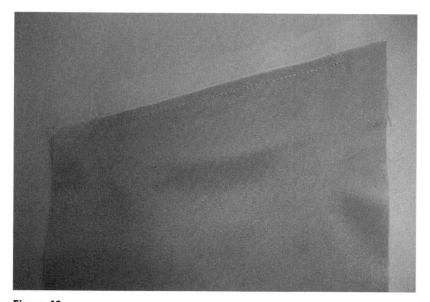

Figure 40

6. Butt the longest pocket bag (BACK) to the edge of the first pocket bag, as shown below, and sew using a 5mm seam width. Reduce the seam length by 5mm at each end.
   Back-tack at the beginning and end of the seam (see Figure 41).

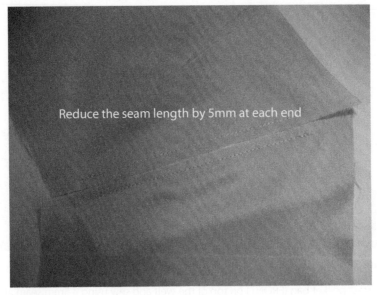

Figure 41

7. Cut between the two lines of stitching (finishing approximately 1cm from the end of the shortest row of stitching). Mitre the corners, forming the fish tails (see Figure 42).

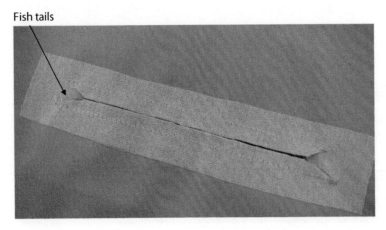

Figure 42

8. Push the pocket bags through to the inside of the garment. Turn to the right side of the garment and stitch the ends of the welt to the garment using a 2mm seam width. Back-tack at the beginning and end of the seam (see Figure 43).

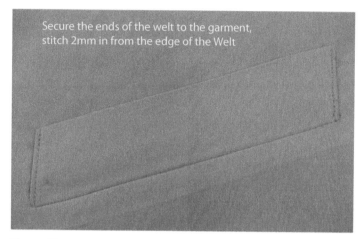

Secure the ends of the welt to the garment, stitch 2mm in from the edge of the Welt

Figure 43

9. Sew around the pocket bag (see Figure 44).

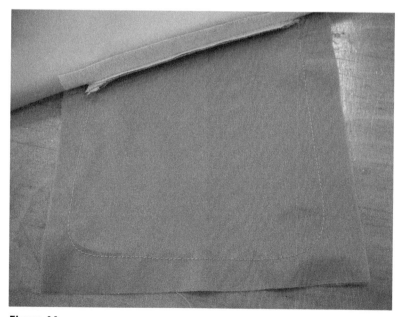

Figure 44

A demonstration of inserting patch, slanted, jetted and welt pockets can be viewed online at www .wiley.com.

CHAPTER 11

SLEEVE OPENING CONSTRUCTION

When a sleeve has a cuff that fastens, some kind of opening in the end of the sleeve is created. There are a variety of constructions, from a bound opening to a gauntlet opening.

In general, men's shirts have a gauntlet opening and ladies' garments such as blouses have a less complex construction, the **bound opening**, often known as a **bound vent**.

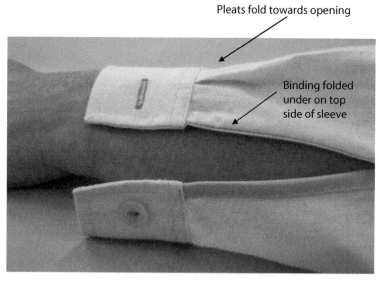

Pleats fold towards opening

Binding folded under on top side of sleeve

Figure 1

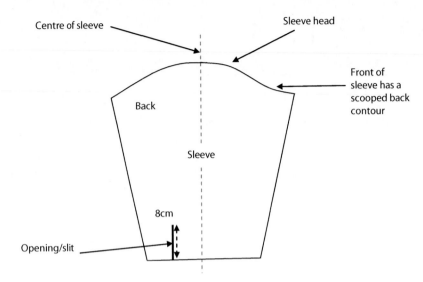

Figure 2

The top of the sleeve, the part that is sewn into the armhole, is called the **sleeve head**.

Identify the front and back of the sleeve head. The front of the sleeve head will be identified by having a slightly greater curved shape than that of the back.

At the bottom of the sleeve, a slit, usually 8cm in length, is cut into the back section of the sleeve. See the diagram above. Cut a strip of binding 2.5cm wide. If the binding is cut from woven fabric, it should be cut on the bias, at a 45° angle across the fabric (see Figure 5).

1. Using the Lockstitch (301), attach the binding to the sleeve opening/slit. The binding can be applied using a folder attachment.

Figure 4   Simplified seam diagram.

Figure 3

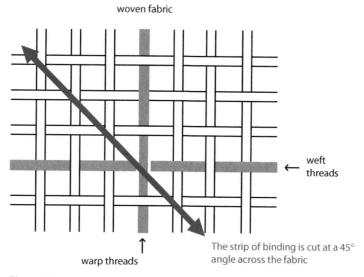

woven fabric

weft threads ←

↑ warp threads

The strip of binding is cut at a 45° angle across the fabric

Figure 5

Alternatively, position the sleeve (correct side of the sleeve facing up) on top of the binding and attach the binding using a 5mm seam allowance using the Lockstitch (301), but only catch the fabric at the top of the sleeve slit with the minimum seam allowance (see Figure 6).

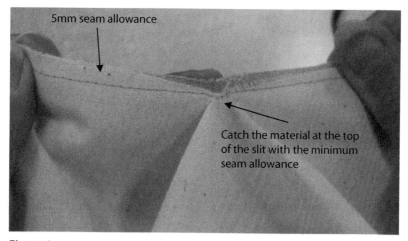

5mm seam allowance

Catch the material at the top of the slit with the minimum seam allowance

Figure 6

2. Fold under the raw edge of the binding (5mm), then fold it around the raw fabric edge of the slit and stitch into position using the Lockstitch.

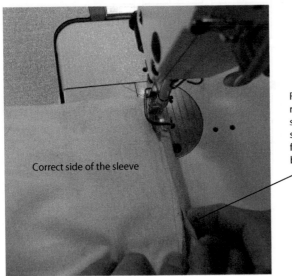

Correct side of the sleeve

Fold under the binding raw edge (5mm) and secure in position, stitching 1 mm from the folded edge of the binding

Figure 7

Figure 8   Simplified seam diagram.

Figure 9   Bound slit opening.

3. Turn the sleeve to the wrong side and mitre the binding at the top of the opening slit. Back-tack at the start and end of the seam (see Figure 11).

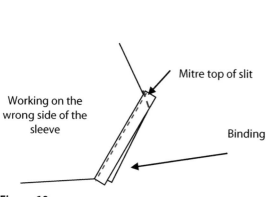

Mitre top of slit

Working on the wrong side of the sleeve

Binding

Figure 10

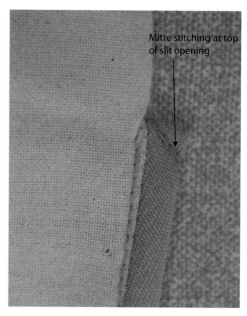

Mitre stitching at top of slit opening

Figure 11

4. Turn the sleeve to the wrong side facing up, fold binding on the front section of the sleeve towards the underarm seam and tack binding back using a 5mm seam allowance.

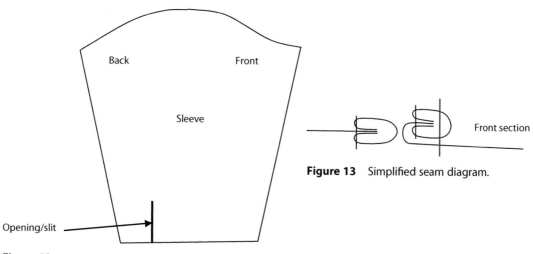

Back　　　　Front

Sleeve

Front section

Figure 13　Simplified seam diagram.

Opening/slit

Figure 12

Gauntlet Opening

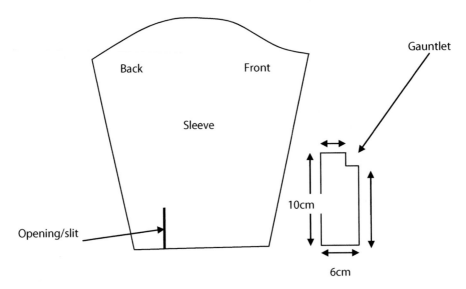

Figure 14

Figure 15

1. With the wrong side of the sleeve facing up and using the Lockstitch (301), neaten the side of the slit nearest to the sleeve underarm seam by double turn hemming (5mm) and tapering to nothing at the top of the slit (see Figure 16).

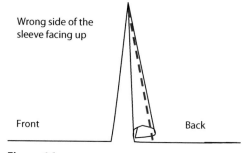

Figure 16

2. Attach the shortest side of the gauntlet to the other side of the slit using the Lockstitch (301), taking a 5mm seam allowance width (see Figure 17).

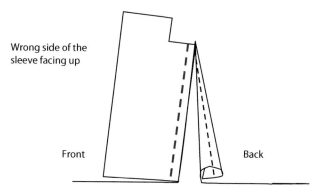

Figure 17

3. Turn to the correct side of the sleeve, fold the gauntlet around the raw seam edges and stitch in position as illustrated, turning in the top edge to fold the box.

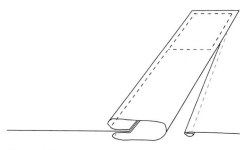

Figure 18

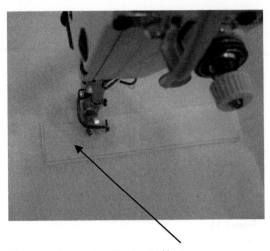

The top of the opening slit is located here
under the placket, therefore the final row
of stitching must catch both sides of the
opening below this point.

Figure 19

The shape of the placket and stitching can be decorative, see Figure 20.

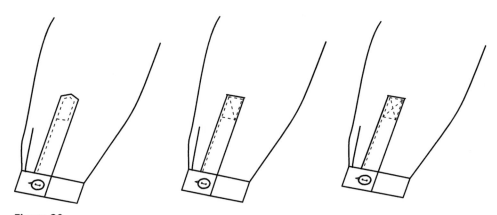

Figure 20

A demonstration of constructing sleeve openings can be viewed online at www.wiley.com.

CHAPTER 12
ASSEMBLING & ATTACHING CUFFS

Sleeves can be finished with a simple hem or a cuff can be used to provide a finished edge to the sleeve; cuffs can be found in a variety of styles.

Cuffs at the wrist that do not have a fastening must be big enough to easily go over the broadest part of the hand.

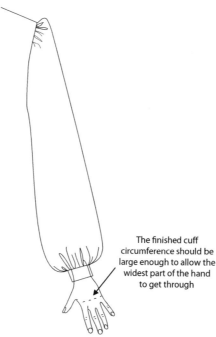

The finished cuff circumference should be large enough to allow the widest part of the hand to get through

Figure 1

Cuffs on short sleeves should have enough ease allowance for the bicep when it is flexed.

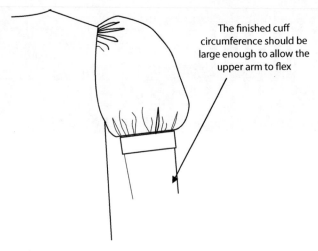

The finished cuff circumference should be large enough to allow the upper arm to flex

Figure 2

TWO PIECE CUFF

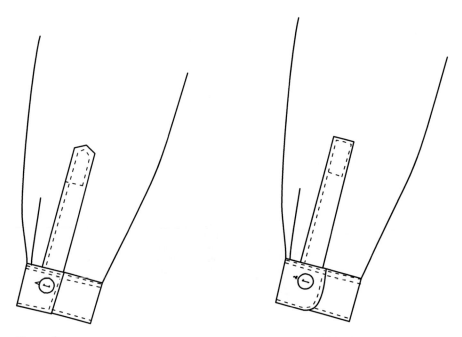

Figure 3

This type of cuff is frequently used on men's shirts and women's blouses. The ends of the cuffs can be curved or straight.

Suggested dimensions for a cuff on a man's shirt:

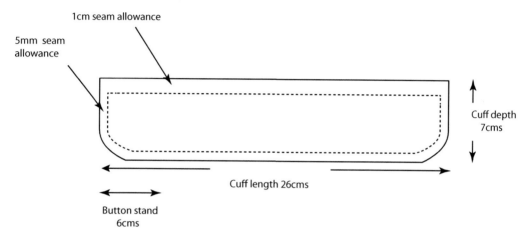

Figure 4

Each cuff is made from two pieces.

1. Fuse interlining to the wrong side of the outer cuff piece but exclude the seam allowances.

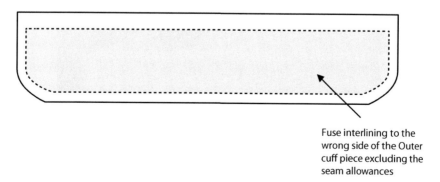

Figure 5

2. Working with the wrong side of the outer cuff, turn of 1cm of the top edge over the interlining and stitch with the Lockstitch (301) using a 5mm seam width (see Figure 6).

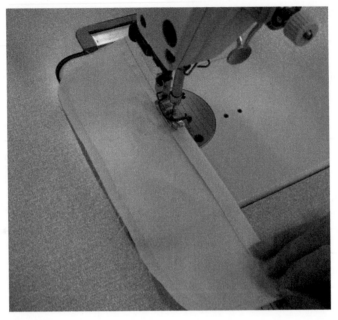

Figure 6

3. Align the outer and inner cuff pieces together with the correct sides facing and join the two pieces using the Lockstitch (301) stitch, as illustrated. Use the edge of the interlining as a guide to stitch around (see Figure 7a).

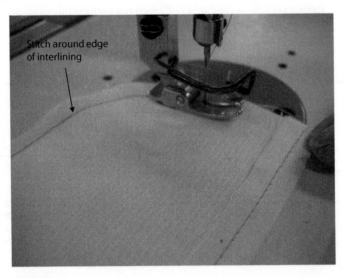

Stitch around edge of interlining

Figure 7a

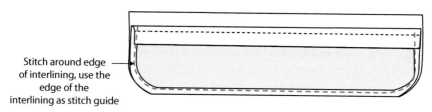

Stitch around edge
of interlining, use the
edge of the
interlining as stitch guide

Figure 7b

4. Turn the cuff through to the correct side and, with the correct side of the cuff up, topstitch. See Figure 8, start and finish 1cm from the folded edge.

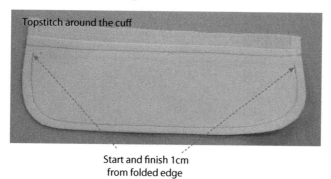

Topstitch around the cuff

Start and finish 1cm
from folded edge

Figure 8

ONE PIECE CUFF

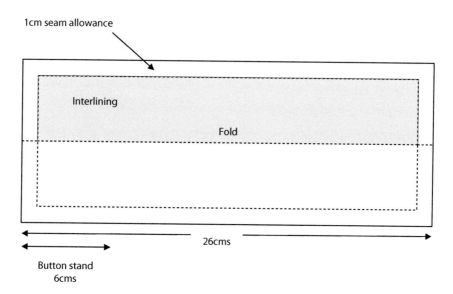

1cm seam allowance

Interlining

Fold

26cms

Button stand
6cms

Figure 9

This cuff is cut from one piece of fabric, see the suggested dimensions in Figure 9 for a cuff on a man's shirt.

1. Fuse the interlining to the wrong side of the outer cuff section but exclude the seam allowances.
2. Turn the top edge over the interlining and, using the Lockstitch (301), stitch with a 5mm seam width.

Figure 10

3. Fold the cuff, with the correct sides of the fabric together; the raw top edge should extend by 1cm. Using the Lockstitch (301), stitch both ends, back-tacking at the start and end of the seam.

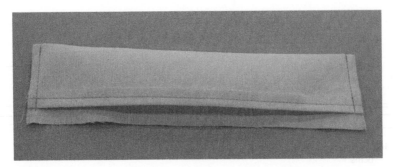

Figure 11

4. Turn the cuff through to the right side and press.

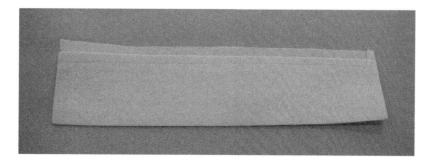

Figure 12

ATTACHING THE CUFF TO THE SLEEVE

1. Join the sleeve underarm seam.
2. Turn the sleeve to the correct side, place the cuff inside the sleeve, align the raw edge of the cuff with the bottom of the sleeve and align each end of the cuff with the sleeve opening edges. Fold excess sleeve fullness into one or more pleats. The pleat folds should face towards the opening when the garment is worn. Attach the cuff edge onto the sleeve end using the Lockstitch (301).

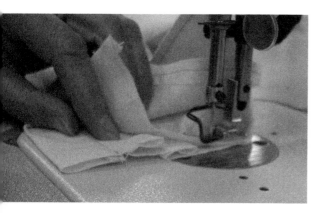

Figure 13

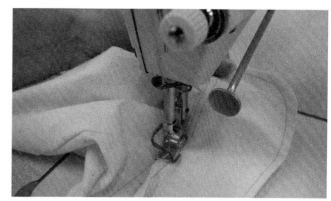

Figure 14

3. Working on the correct side of the garment, tuck the raw edges of the sleeve into the cuff and close the outside cuff onto the sleeve by stitching 1mm from the edge.

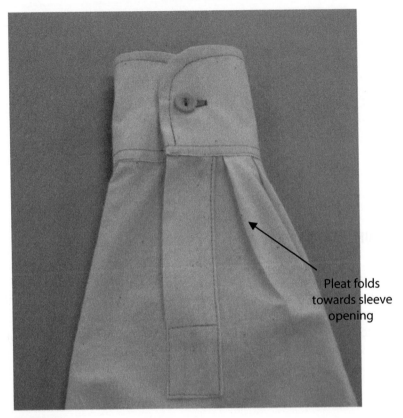

Pleat folds towards sleeve opening

Figure 15

4. Finally, insert a buttonhole and attach the button.

A demonstration of constructing cuffs and attaching a cuff can be viewed online at www.wiley.com.

CHAPTER 13
ASSEMBLING & ATTACHING COLLARS

Collars come in a variety of shapes, from a simple collar such as the stand collar, frequently known as a Mandarin, to a more complex collar such as a shirt collar. Each collar style will require a particular method of assembly and application to the neckline and front opening finish.

COLLAR PARTS

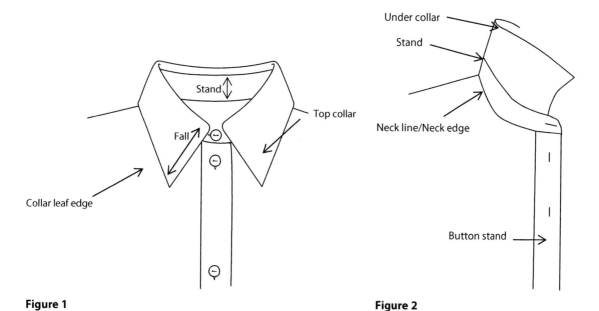

Figure 1

Figure 2

The under collar pattern should be slightly smaller than the top collar. As a general rule, the under collar should be 5mm smaller when cut from bulky fabrics and 2mm smaller when cut from medium to light-weight fabrics. Having the top collar larger enables the leaf edge seam of the collar to roll under.

A fusible interfacing should be applied to the top collar excluding the seam allowances. This will provide stability and shape to the collar. Select an interlining that is the same or lighter in weight than the fabric that the collar and garment are made from. When using knitted or stretch fabrics, select an interfacing that gives when the fabric is stretched.

STAND COLLAR (FREQUENTLY KNOWN AS THE MANDARIN COLLAR)

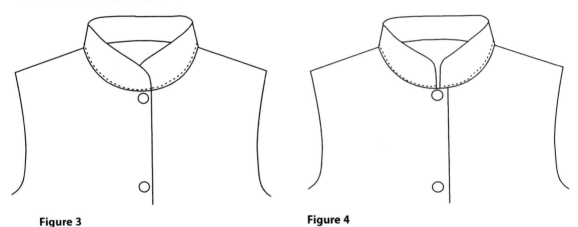

Figure 3   **Figure 4**

The collar ends can be curved or straight. The collar can be cut to the same length as the garment neckline; when the garment is closed the collar ends will overlap, as seen in the first illustration. The second collar illustrates a collar with the collar ends cut to come to the centre front of the garment only.

1.   Create the garment neckline by joining both shoulder seams. Neaten the front edges using the Three Thread Overedge (504). Make a simple button stand by turning the button stand to the inside and press into position.
2.   Fuse interlining to the wrong side of the top collar piece only but exclude the seam

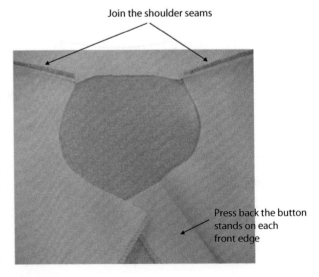

Join the shoulder seams

Press back the button stands on each front edge

Figure 5

allowances. Working with the wrong side of the top collar facing uppermost, turn 1cm of the bottom edge over the interlining and stitch with the Lockstitch (301) using a 5mm seam width (see Figures 6 and 7).

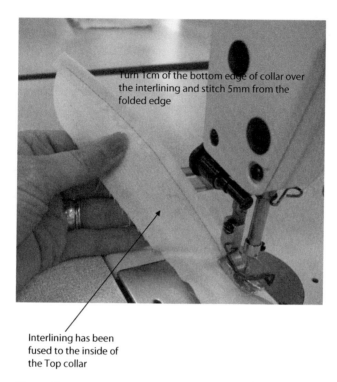

Turn 1cm of the bottom edge of collar over the interlining and stitch 5mm from the folded edge

Interlining has been fused to the inside of the Top collar

Figure 6

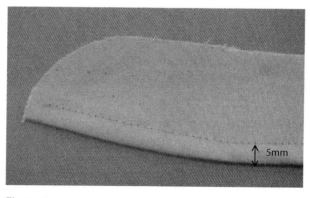

5mm

Figure 7

3.   Align the top and under collar pieces together with the correct sides facing and join the two pieces. Using the Lockstitch (301), stitch as illustrated, taking a 5mm seam allowance. Use the edge of the interlining as a guide to stitch around (see Figure 8).

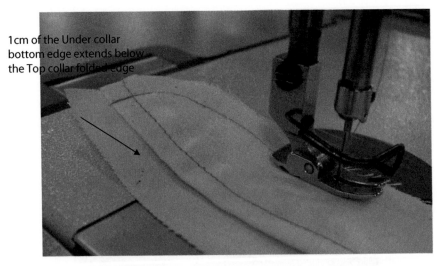

1cm of the Under collar bottom edge extends below the Top collar folded edge

Figure 8

4.   Turn the collar through to the right side and press. The collar can now be attached to the garment neckline.

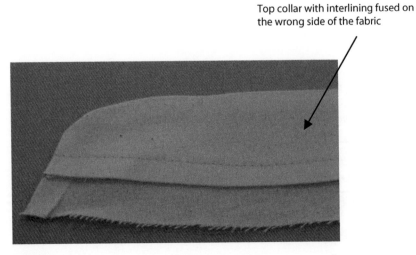

Top collar with interlining fused on the wrong side of the fabric

Figure 9

ATTACHING THE STAND COLLAR

5.   Place the bottom raw edge of the under collar to the neckline. The under collar must be placed on top of the wrong side of the garment. Align the collar neckline and garment neckline and sew using the Lockstitch (301), taking a 1cm seam allowance but avoiding catching the top collar bottom edge when sewing this seam. The notches on the edge of the collar must align with the shoulder seams.

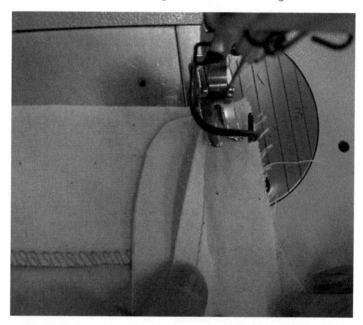

Figure 10

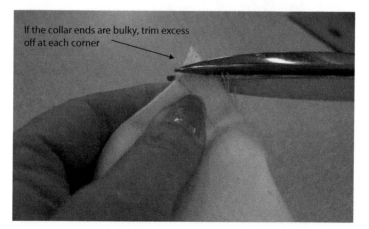

Figure 11   If the collar ends are bulky, trim excess off at each corner.

6. Working on the right side of the garment, tuck the raw edge of the neckline into the collar and secure the bottom folded edge of the collar onto the garment by stitching 1mm from the edge using the Lockstitch (301). See Figures 12 and 13 below.

Figure 12

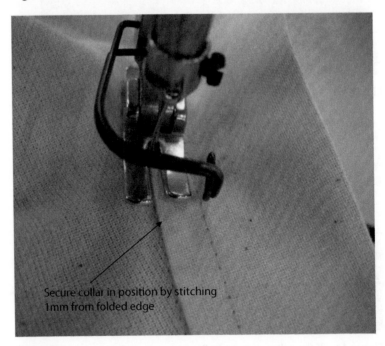

Secure collar in position by stitching 1mm from folded edge

Figure 13

7. Finally, insert the buttonholes and attach the buttons.

FLAT COLLAR (ALSO KNOWN AS THE PETER PAN COLLAR)

The collar ends can be rounded or square.

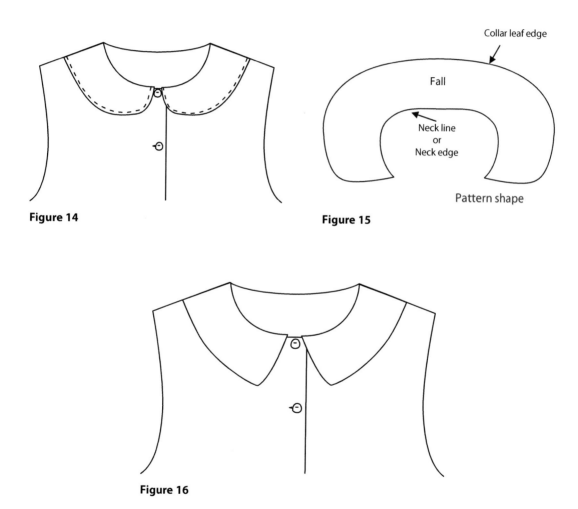

Figure 14

Figure 15

Figure 16

1. Create the garment neckline by joining both shoulder seams. Make a simple button stand, turn the button stand to the inside and press into position.

2. Fuse interlining to the wrong side of the top collar piece but exclude the seam allowances.
    Place the correct sides of the top collar and under collar together, align the leaf edges and, using the
    Lockstitch (301), join both collar pieces together around the leaf edge using a 5mm seam allowance.

Figure 17

3. Turn the collar through to the right side and press. The collar can now be topstitched.

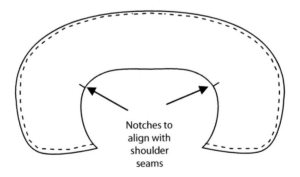

Notches to
align with
shoulder
seams

Figure 18

4. The collar can now be attached to the garment neckline.

ATTACHING THE FLAT COLLAR

5. Create the garment neckline by joining both shoulder seams. Neaten the front edges using the Three Thread Overedge (504). Make a simple button stand by turning the button stand to the inside and press into position.

6. Working on the correct side of the garment, with the top collar facing uppermost, align the raw neck edge of the collar with the neck edge of the garment. Position the collar ends at the notches indicating the centre front line (see Figure 19).

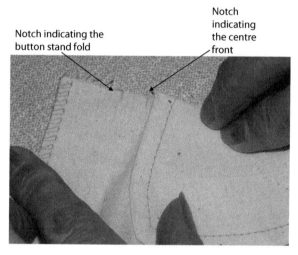

Notch indicating the button stand fold

Notch indicating the centre front

Figure 19

Fold the button stand over the collar and, using the Lockstitch (301), take a 1cm seam allowance and join the collar onto the neckline, back-tacking at the beginning and end of the seam (see Figures 20 and 21).

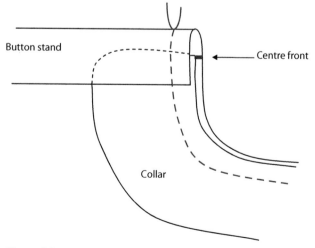

Button stand

Centre front

Collar

Figure 20

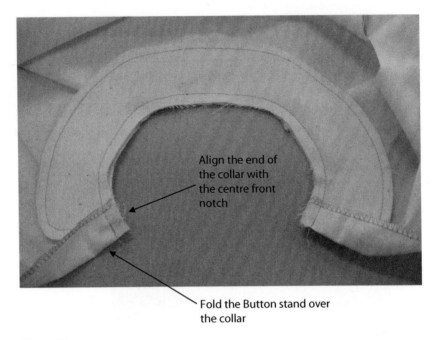

Align the end of the collar with the centre front notch

Fold the Button stand over the collar

Figure 21

7. Use the Three Thread Overedge (504) to neaten the seam edge.

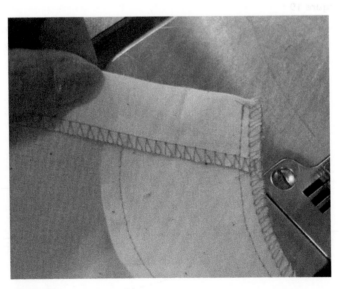

Figure 22

8. Turn the button stands through and, working with the correct side of the garment uppermost, now use the Lockstitch (301) to topstitch the collar joining seam flat.

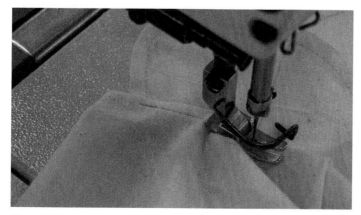

Figure 23

9. Finally, insert buttonholes and attach the buttons.

ONE-PIECE SHIRT COLLAR

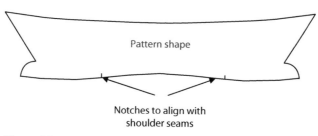

Pattern shape

Notches to align with
shoulder seams

Figure 24

Figure 25

1.   Fuse interlining to the wrong side of the top collar but exclude the seam allowances.

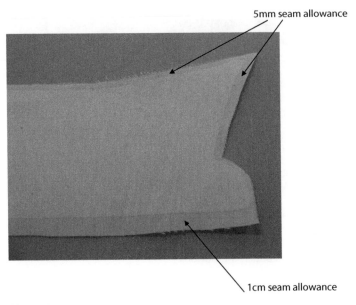

5mm seam allowance

1cm seam allowance

Figure 26

2.   Work with the wrong side of the top collar, turn the bottom edge over the interlining and stitch with the Lockstitch (301) using a 5mm seam width (see Figure 27).

Figure 27

3. Align the top and under collar pieces together with the correct sides facing and join the two pieces. Using the Lockstitch (301), take a 5mm seam allowance and back-tack at the beginning and end of the seam. Use the edge of the interlining as a guide to stitch around.

Figure 28

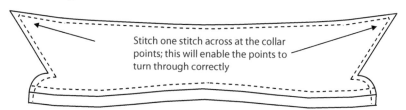

Stitch one stitch across at the collar points; this will enable the points to turn through correctly

Figure 29

4. Cut into the stitching and trim points as shown (see Figures 30 and 31).

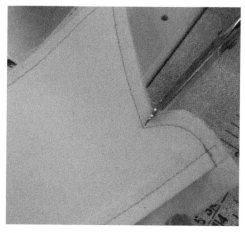

Figure 30

Figure 31

5. Turn the collar through to the right side and, with the top collar facing up, topstitch.

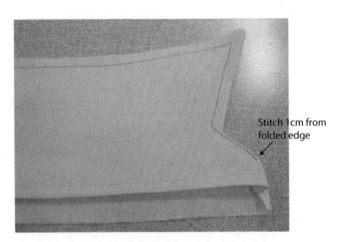

Stitch 1cm from folded edge

Figure 32

ATTACHING THE SHIRT COLLAR

6. Create the garment neckline by joining both shoulder seams. Create a button stand on the front edges.
7. Working on the correct side of the garment, with the top collar facing uppermost, align the raw neck edge of the collar with the neck edge of the garment. Using the Lockstitch (301), take a 1cm seam allowance; stitch the upper collar onto the neckline of the garment taking care **not** to catch the top collar in this seam (see Figure 33).

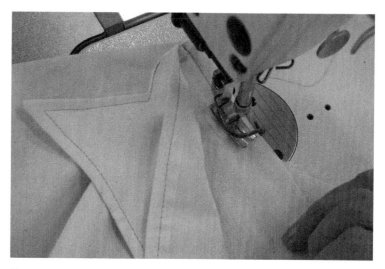

Figure 33

8. Working on the wrong side of the garment, tuck the raw edge of the neckline into the collar and secure the bottom folded edge of the top collar onto the garment by stitching 1mm from the edge using the Lockstitch (301).

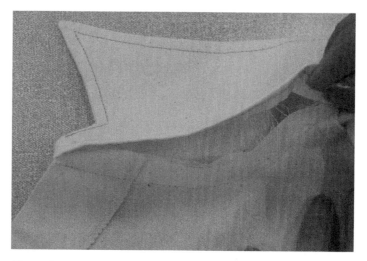

Figure 34

9. Finally, insert buttonholes and attach the buttons.

A demonstration of constructing Peter Pan, stand and shirt collars and attaching them onto a garment neckline can be viewed online at www.wiley.com.

CHAPTER 14

SEWING PROBLEMS

The problems which arise when materials are sewn vary in their seriousness. Some only cause minor appearance problems, which are negligible in low cost garments, whilst others cause damage to the material, which is impossible to repair and therefore renders the garment useless.

The main problems are:

1. Problems in stitch formation, which give rise to poor seam appearance and performance.
2. Problems of fabric distortion known as pucker, which also give rise to poor seam appearance.
3. Damage to the fabric along the stitch line.

STITCH FORMATION PROBLEMS

Skipped stitches are caused by the failure of the needle to enter the lower thread loop at the correct time. See Figure 1 for the Two Needle Chainstitch Bottom Cover (406); this fault will result in the stitch easily unravelling. Skipped stitches can be minimised by properly maintaining the stitch-forming mechanism in the sewing machine.

All thread tensions should be as light as possible; this will enable the needle thread and the bobbin thread to link in the middle of the fabric plies as shown in Figure 2.

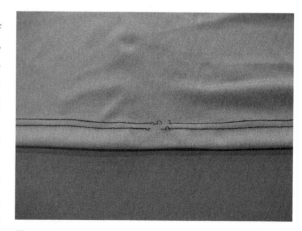

Figure 1

Figure 2

Improper stitch balance occurs if the tension is too tight on either the bobbin or needle thread; loops will be seen either on the underside or topside of the seam. When the threads do not link in the middle of the fabric plies, the seam will break when the seam is subjected to strain. This problem can be resolved by properly balancing the stitch tensions, so that the needle and bobbin threads meet in the middle of the seam.

Figure 3 shows improperly balanced stitches: the tension on the needle thread is too tight.

Figure 3

Seam grin will result when there is insufficient tension on the threads forming the seam and the stitches will open on the face side of the garment when the seam is subjected to strain (see Figure 4).

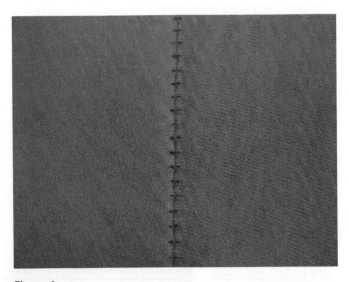

Figure 4

To resolve this problem, readjust the sewing machine thread tensions so that a proper stitch balance is achieved. It should be noted that too much tension can cause problems including seam failure, stitch cracking and excessive thread breakage and skipped stitches.

An **inconsistent edge** on an Overedge stitch is when the edge of the fabric either appears to be rolled or ragged inside the stitch. This is caused by the knife in the Overedge machine being blunt or incorrectly positioned in relation to the 'stitch tongue' on the needle plate to obtain the proper seam width.

FABRIC DISTORTION – PUCKER

Pucker is a wrinkled appearance along a seam length. Generally, there appears to be too much fabric and not enough thread in the seam or it appears that the thread is drawing up the fabric.

Pucker can be caused by the incorrect seam construction, incorrect needle size, incorrect thread size, poor tension control and poor feed control or by the fabric structure.

Pucker may not show itself when the garment is first sewn, but pucker can occur after the garment has been pressed using steam or laundered (see Figure 5).

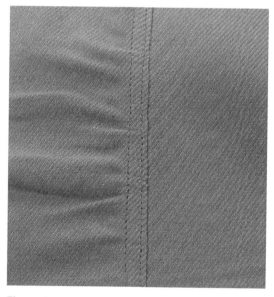

Figure 5

Pucker Types

Feed puckering appears as a result of the fabric plies in the seam not being aligned properly during the sewing process. The two plies of fabric are not being transported through the machine at the same pace. The lower fabric ply is transported at a faster speed as it is in direct contact with the feed dogs.

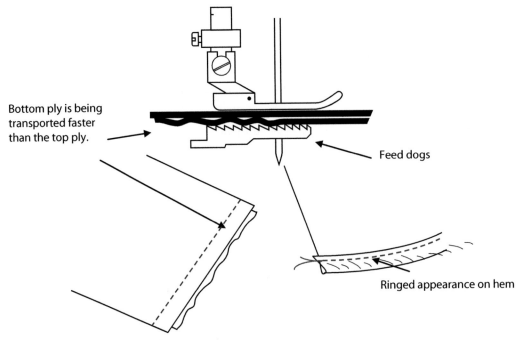

Bottom ply is being transported faster than the top ply.

Feed dogs

Ringed appearance on hem

Figure 6

All Overedge machines have positive top and bottom feed systems, therefore the bottom feed can be adjusted to resolve this problem and improve fabric handling when sewing.

Tension puckering appears when the threads have been stretched and sewn into the seam. The thread then causes the seam to draw back and pucker. Too much tension has been applied to the threads, thereby causing a stretch in the thread. After sewing, the thread relaxes. When it recovers to its original length, it gathers up the seam. This type of pucker is often referred to as seam shrinkage.

This problem can be resolved by reducing thread tension to as light as possible but maintaining a balanced stitch. If the problem continues, consider changing the sewing thread and applying a low-friction lubricant.

Yarn displacement or **structural jamming** is caused by sewing seams with too large a thread size that causes the yarns in the seam to be displaced, giving a puckered appearance. In this case, the presence of the thread in the seam itself introduces distortion and the pucker has nothing to do with the sewing machine. This can occur in very closely and densely woven fabrics, as there is little to no space left between the yarns in either the warp or weft direction of the fabric, making it extremely difficult or impossible to force in another thread in either direction. This results directly from the action of jamming an extra thread into the structure, which is already too closely set to accommodate it.

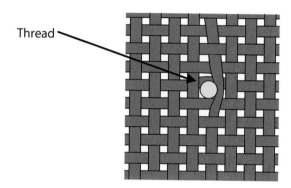

Figure 7

The problem can be resolved by using a smaller size thread with a higher tenacity, smaller size needle and reducing the number of stitches in the seam. If the pucker occurs whilst using a Lockstitch (301), consider changing the stitch type to the Two Thread Chainstitch (401). The threads in this stitch link on the underside of the fabric and therefore reduce a build-up of threads in the middle of the fabric, which can alleviate seam pucker. If possible, cut the garment on the bias (cross-grain) of the fabric, as this will open up space between the yarns to enable the thread to be accommodated.

DAMAGE TO THE FABRIC

Damage may be caused by a faulty needle or by using the incorrect needle type. Using the incorrect needle type or a damaged needle can result in the needle striking and breaking the yarns in the fabric structure.

Needle damage is especially serious in knitted fabrics, as they will ladder if damaged. The damage is often not apparent when first sewn; it only becomes evident when the garment is worn or washed, causing the broken yarn to run back and become visible (see Figure 8).

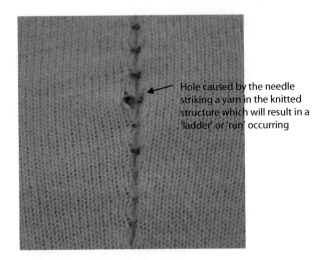

Hole caused by the needle striking a yarn in the knitted structure which will result in a 'ladder' or 'run' occurring

Figure 8

Ensure the correct thread size and needle type and size are being used for the fabric; for example, a ball point needle should be used when sewing knitted fabrics.

Needle heat occurs as a result of friction between the needle and fabric being sewn. During high-speed sewing, a needle can reach temperatures of up to 400 °C (as covered in Chapter 4). Natural fabrics can withstand these temperatures for a short time but synthetic fabrics or synthetic coated fabrics will melt:

⇒ **PVC fibres** will melt around 100 °C.
⇒ **Polyamide and Polyester** soften at 230 °C.
⇒ **Poly Acrylics** soften at 280 °C.

Overheated needles can soften fibres, thereby weakening them and producing rough seam lines with harsh stitch holes. The melted fibres stick to the needle and eventually clog up the eye of the needle, preventing the thread from passing and then the thread will break.

High-speed industrial sewing machines sew at very high speeds from 4000 to 10,000 stitches per minute, causing friction between the needle blade and the fabric. Other factors, such as fabric thickness and finish, fabric colour (darker colours are normally worse than lighter colours), needle size and length, needle surface finish and, in particular, using synthetic threads to sew synthetic fabrics, can cause excessive thread breakage and damage to the fabric being sewn when needle heat is generated.

Generally, needle heat causes thread breakage when the machinist stops sewing after a long run and the thread comes to rest in the needle eye. The result may be that polyester or nylon thread will melt and break.

The problem can be resolved by putting a lubricant on the thread to help minimise needle heat or using needle coolers or devices that blow compressed air onto the needle during sewing.

Seam failure is where the yarns in the fabric pull out of the seam from the edge. This can occur on fabrics made from continuous filament yarns that are very smooth and have a slippery surface or when a woven fabric is loosely woven.

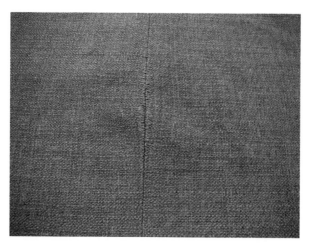

Figure 9a

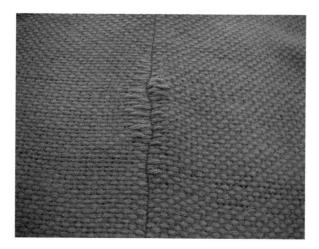

Figure 9b

To reduce this problem, consider using a French seam or lapped felled seam construction or, alternatively, increase the seam width.

GARMENT ASSEMBLY TERMS GLOSSARY

Back-tacking   Back-tacking is sewing in reverse and forward over the same stitches to secure a line of sewing; this can be done at the beginning and the end of a seam to prevent the stitching from unravelling.

Ball point needle   The point of the needle is designed to penetrate knit fabrics without cutting or damaging the fabric.

Bar tack   A group of closely sewn 304, Zig Zag stitches used to reinforce stress points on garments such as pocket mouth corners and attach belt loops.

Bound/binding   A strip of fabric cut on the bias (cut at 45° to the straight grain of the fabric) which is used to finish off/neaten the raw edge on a garment such as an armhole.

Cone of thread   A large package of thread which holds 5000+ metres of thread.

Cop of thread   A medium size package of thread which holds approximately 1000 metres of thread.

Dart   A wedge removed from the garment by stitching to create shape, such as creating fullness in the bust area of a garment. Darts can also be placed to achieve fit and creative design features.

Face side   The correct side of the fabric/garment.

Hem   The raw edge is turned under or over and sewn to neaten the edge of the garment, such as the bottom edge of a shirt.

Pin tuck   A narrow fold/pleat secured by topstitching which provides a decorative feature on a garment.

Press   Using an iron to apply pressure with or without steam to impart a flat appearance to a seam, fabrics or garments or introduce desired creases in garments.

Raw edge   The edge of the fabric that is not stitched or finished.

Seam   The joining of two or more layers of fabric that are held together by sewing or welding.

Seam allowance   The amount of fabric between the stitching and raw edge.

Seam pucker   Refers to the gathering of a seam during sewing after sewing or after laundering, causing an unacceptable seam appearance.

Stitch bight   The distance between the inner edge of the stitch and the adjacent edge of the stitch. This term is commonly used to describe the Overedge stitch width.

Tack   A temporary stitch to hold pieces together, usually removed after final stitching. Tacking is frequently referred to as basting.

Topstitch   Exposed stitching which is sewn a uniform distance from a load-bearing seam. Mainly used to strengthen the seam and give a decorative appearance. Topstitching can be done in the same or contrasting thread, depending on the desired decorative effect required.

Under side   The wrong side of the fabric/garment.

Welding   Seam welding is a process which joins two similar fabrics together. The seam may be a butt join or an overlap join and may use one of three methods:

Ultrasonic joining, where high-frequency vibrations bond together two or more materials, which are predominantly made from a synthetic composition, such as 100%, acrylic, polyester, nylon, polyethylene, polypropylene and some polyvinyl chloride or blends of these with up to 35% natural fibres. Ultrasonic techniques can be used to cut, sew and seal materials. Ultrasonic assembly converts high frequency electrical energy into high frequency sound vibrations that are transmitted under pressure. This creates heat, melts the fabric and within seconds of the material cooling, a molecular bond between the two parts is formed.

Hot plate welding uses a metal plate heated by electrodes to transfer heat to the material, which in turn melts the material and creates the bond.

Adhesive joining, as the name suggests, is where a sticky substance is used to join the seam. This sticky substance is usually transferred from a silicone paper or a similar material into the seam. The sticky substance is melted by means of heat to join the seam.

AUTHOR

Jayne Smith has worked in the fashion industry for over 30 years. Her passion for fashion assembly led her to deliver this discipline at the Scottish College of Textiles and the School of Textiles and Design, Heriot-Watt University, Scotland. A Senior Teaching Fellow, she held the position of Director of Learning & Teaching in the school for many years and was responsible for developing and implementing the overall learning and teaching strategy, which equipped students with a portfolio of key skills to succeed in the global fashion industry.

She is a talented Product Developer, specialising in assembly and creative pattern cutting for fashion. Her expertise in this subject has led her to deliver the discipline in many universities and colleges across Europe, Scandinavia, Ireland, Turkey, Vietnam, Dubai and China.

Prior to her career in academia, she was a Garment Technologist and Pattern Cutter for the Courtaulds Group, responsible for the development of design ideas to a commercial status for manufacture for customers and a Designer for Glen Abbey in Ireland. She has also run her own successful business, Sarah Jayne Childrenswear.

Born in Ireland, Jayne graduated from Belfast Metropolitan College with a diploma from the Clothing & Footwear Institute followed by a BA (Hons) in Clothing from Manchester Metropolitan University, Hollings Faculty.

Her product development and pattern-cutting expertise has been applied to a range of consultancy work, from designing and implementing short courses in pattern cutting and garment assembly to managing a variety of consultancy garment technology projects for the fashion industry.

INDEX

Printed and bound by CPI Group (UK) Ltd, Croydon, CR0 4YY

07/11/2024

14587813-0001